SCHOLASTIC

National Curriculum

Maths

Practice Book for

Year 5

SCHOLASTIC

Book End, Range Road, Witney, Oxfordshire, OX29 0YD
www.scholastic.co.uk

1 2 3 4 5 6 7 8 9   4 5 6 7 8 9 0 1 2 3

British Library Cataloguing-in-Publication Data
A catalogue record for this book is available from the British Library.

ISBN 978-1407-12892-4
Printed and bound in India by Replika Press Pvt. Ltd.

Editorial
Rachel Morgan, Robin Hunt, Kate Baxter, Jenny Penfold, Lucy Tritton

Design
Scholastic Design Team: Neil Salt, Nicolle Thomas
and Oxford Designers & Illustrators Ltd

Cover Design
Dipa Mistry

Cover Illustration
James W Hunter

Illustration
Tomek.gr

Contents

Why buy this book?

The *100 Practice Activities* series has been designed to support the National Curriculum in schools in England. The curriculum is challenging in mathematics and includes the requirement for children's understanding to be secure before moving on. These practice books will help your child revise and practise all of the skills they will learn at school, including some topics they might not have encountered previously.

How to use this book

- The content is divided into National Curriculum topics (for example, Addition and subtraction, Fractions and so on). Find out what your child is doing in school and dip into the relevant practice activities as required. The index at the back of the book will help you to identify appropriate topics.
- Share the activities and support your child if necessary using the helpful quick tips at the top of most pages.
- Keep the working time short and come back to an activity if your child finds it too difficult. Ask your child to note any areas of difficulty at the back of the book. Don't worry if your child does not 'get' a concept first time, as children learn at different rates and content is likely to be covered throughout the school year.
- Check your child's answers using the answers section on www.scholastic.co.uk/100practice/mathsy5 where you will also find additional interactive activities for your child to play, and some extra resources to support your child's learning (such as number grids and a times tables chart).
- Give lots of encouragement and tick off the progress chart as your child completes each chapter.

How to use the book

This tells you which topic you're working on.

This is the title of the activity.

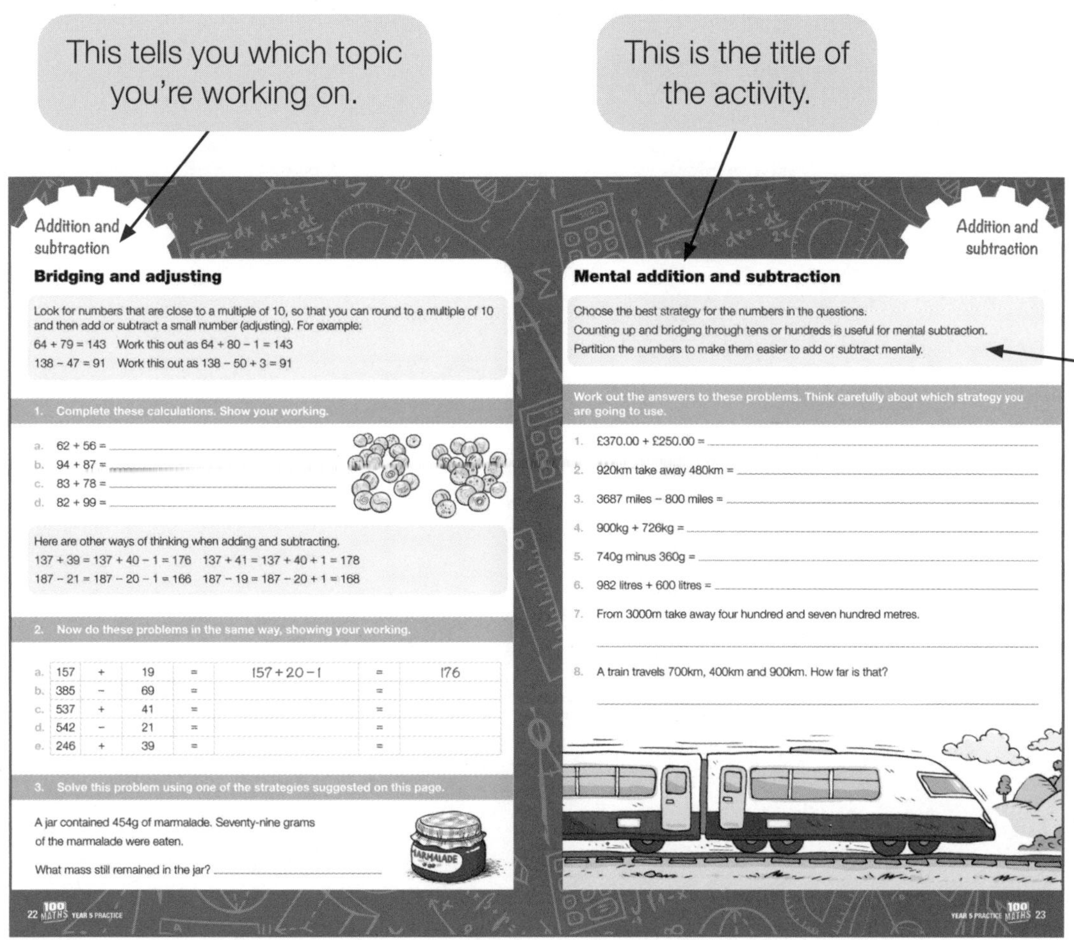

Addition and subtraction

Bridging and adjusting

Look for numbers that are close to a multiple of 10, so that you can round to a multiple of 10 and then add or subtract a small number (adjusting). For example:
64 + 79 = 143 Work this out as 64 + 80 − 1 = 143
138 − 47 = 91 Work this out as 138 − 50 + 3 = 91

1. Complete these calculations. Show your working.

a. 62 + 56 =
b. 94 + 87 =
c. 83 + 78 =
d. 82 + 99 =

Here are other ways of thinking when adding and subtracting.
137 + 39 = 137 + 40 − 1 = 176 137 + 41 = 137 + 40 + 1 = 178
187 − 21 = 187 − 20 − 1 = 166 187 − 19 = 187 − 20 + 1 = 168

2. Now do these problems in the same way, showing your working.

a.	157	+	19	=	157 + 20 − 1	=	176
b.	385	−	69	=		=	
c.	537	+	41	=		=	
d.	542	−	21	=		=	
e.	246	+	39	=		=	

3. Solve this problem using one of the strategies suggested on this page.

A jar contained 454g of marmalade. Seventy-nine grams of the marmalade were eaten.

What mass still remained in the jar?

22 100 MATHS YEAR 5 PRACTICE

Addition and subtraction

Mental addition and subtraction

Choose the best strategy for the numbers in the questions.
Counting up and bridging through tens or hundreds is useful for mental subtraction.
Partition the numbers to make them easier to add or subtract mentally.

Work out the answers to these problems. Think carefully about which strategy you are going to use.

1. £370.00 + £250.00 =
2. 920km take away 480km =
3. 3687 miles − 800 miles =
4. 900kg + 726kg =
5. 740g minus 360g =
6. 982 litres + 600 litres =
7. From 3000m take away four hundred and seven hundred metres.
8. A train travels 700km, 400km and 900km. How far is that?

YEAR 5 PRACTICE 100 MATHS 23

These boxes will help you with the activity. (If there's not one on your page, go back and find the last one.)

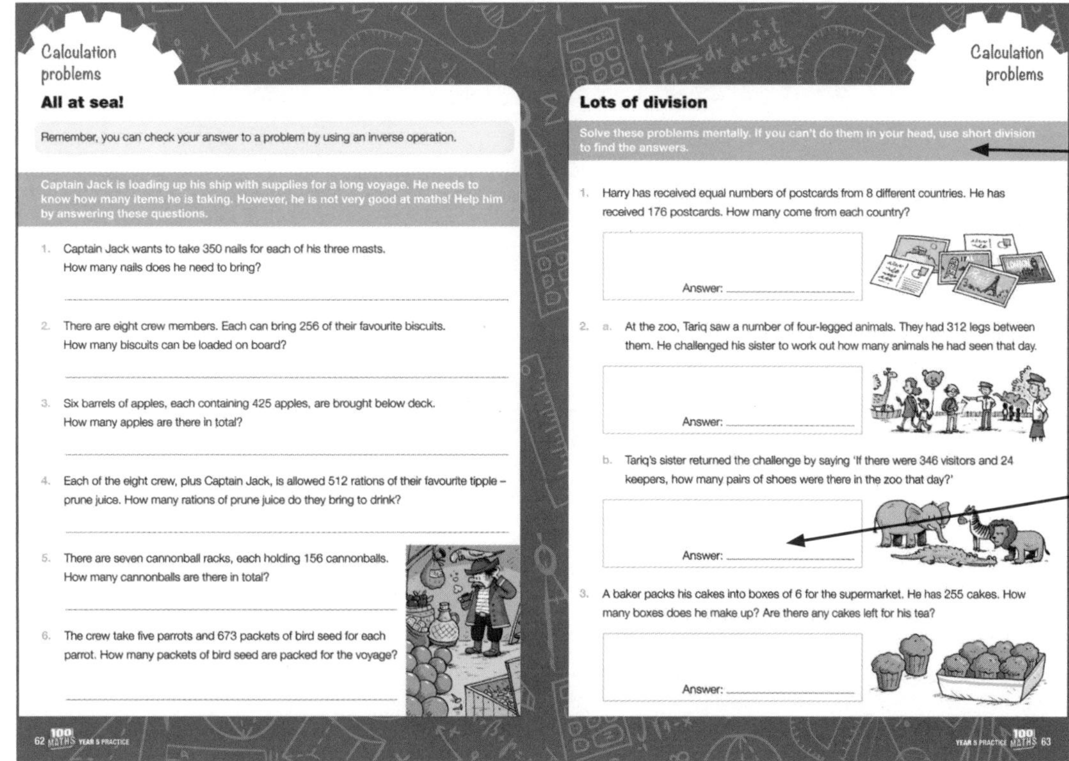

Calculation problems

All at sea!

Remember, you can check your answer to a problem by using an inverse operation.

Captain Jack is loading up his ship with supplies for a long voyage. He needs to know how many items he is taking. However, he is not very good at maths! Help him by answering these questions.

1. Captain Jack wants to take 350 nails for each of his three masts. How many nails does he need to bring?
2. There are eight crew members. Each can bring 256 of their favourite biscuits. How many biscuits can be loaded on board?
3. Six barrels of apples, each containing 425 apples, are brought below deck. How many apples are there in total?
4. Each of the eight crew, plus Captain Jack, is allowed 512 rations of their favourite tipple – prune juice. How many rations of prune juice do they bring to drink?
5. There are seven cannonball racks, each holding 156 cannonballs. How many cannonballs are there in total?
6. The crew take five parrots and 673 packets of bird seed for each parrot. How many packets of bird seed are packed for the voyage?

62 100 MATHS YEAR 5 PRACTICE

Calculation problems

Lots of division

Solve these problems mentally. If you can't do them in your head, use short division to find the answers.

1. Harry has received equal numbers of postcards from 8 different countries. He has received 176 postcards. How many come from each country?
Answer:
2. a. At the zoo, Tariq saw a number of four-legged animals. They had 312 legs between them. He challenged his sister to work out how many animals he had seen that day.
Answer:
b. Tariq's sister returned the challenge by saying 'If there were 346 visitors and 24 keepers, how many pairs of shoes were there in the zoo that day?'
Answer:
3. A baker packs his cakes into boxes of 6 for the supermarket. He has 255 cakes. How many boxes does he make up? Are there any cakes left for his tea?
Answer:

YEAR 5 PRACTICE 100 MATHS 63

This is the instruction text. It tells you what to do.

Follow the instruction to complete the activity.

You might have to write on lines, in boxes, draw or circle things.

If you need help, ask an adult!

Number and place value

Counting in 10s, 100s and 1000s

Take care when you are counting across the 100s and 1000s.

- Count in 10s: 7**9**5, 8**0**5, 8**1**5...
- Count in 100s: 25,**8**84, 25,**9**84, 26,**0**84...
- Count in 1000s: 9**9**,713, 10**0**,713, 10**1**,713...

1. Count forward in 10s from the number at the start until you reach the number at the end.

a. 812 ____ 902

b. 16,157 ____ 16,227

2. Count forward in 100s from the number at the start until you reach the number at the end.

a. 5756 ____ 6656

b. 45,409 ____ 46,109

3. Count back in 100s from the number at the start until you reach the number at the end.

a. 36,554 ____ 35,854

b. 69,228 ____ 68,528

4. Count forward in 1000s from the number at the start until you reach the number at the end.

a. 18,461 ____ 25,461

5. Count back in 1000s from the number at the start until you reach the number at the end.

a. 83,753 ____ 76,753

Counting with negative numbers

Moving in a positive direction means moving forwards along the number line:

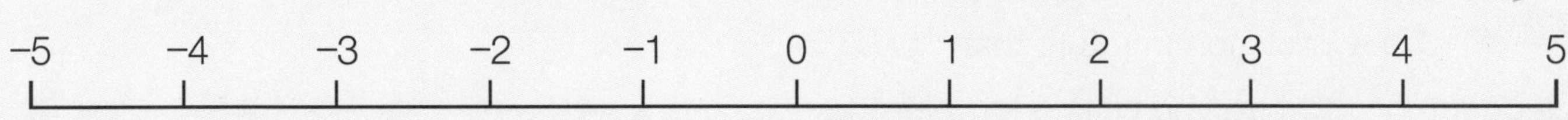

Moving in a negative direction means moving backwards along the number line:

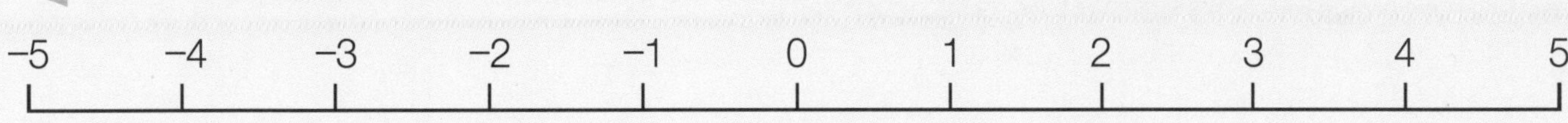

–10 –9 –8 –7 –6 –5 –4 –3 –2 –1 0 1 2 3 4 5 6 7 8 9 10

This is an integer number line.

Numbers on the right-hand side of the line are positive (+) numbers.

Numbers on the left-hand side of the line are negative (–) numbers.

Use the integer number line to help you to solve these problems.

1. Start at –5 and jump eight spaces in a positive direction. Where do you land? __________
2. Start at +3 and jump six spaces in a negative direction. Where do you land? __________
3. Moving in a positive direction, complete these number sequences.
   a. –8, –5, –2, __________, __________, __________, __________
   b. –15, –11, –7, __________, __________, __________, __________
   c. –24, –19, –14, __________, __________, __________, __________
4. Moving in negative direction complete these number sequences.
   a. 15, 10, 5, __________, __________, __________, __________
   b. 13, 10, 7, __________, __________, __________, __________
   c. 22, 15, 8, 1, __________, __________, __________, __________

Negative temperatures

Remember that:

- −5°C is *minus five degrees Celsius*. It is five degrees below zero.
- −10°C is a lower temperature than −5°C.

Include the units when you write a temperature.

Positive and negative numbers are used on a Celsius thermometer scale to show temperatures above and below freezing point (0°C).

Use this thermometer to help you to work out these temperature problems.

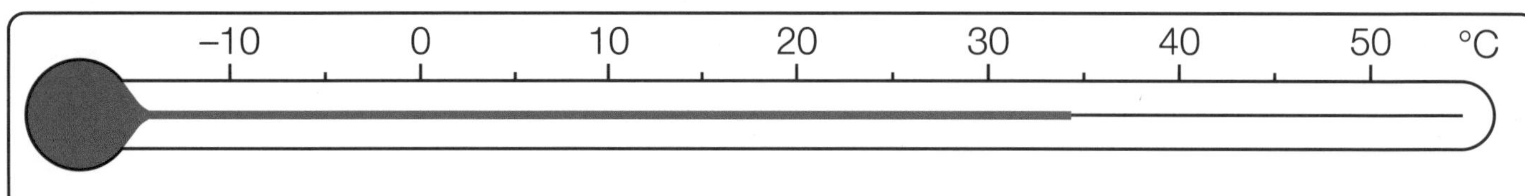

1. By how many degrees has a room's temperature risen if the reading at 9am is –3°C and the 2pm reading is 6°C? ________
2. By how many degrees has the temperature fallen, if the reading at 9am is 2°C and the 2pm reading is –6°C? ________
3. What will the temperature be if there is a rise of 4 degrees from −1°C? ________
4. What will the temperature be if there is a fall of 12 degrees from 7°C? ________
5. What will the temperature be if there is a rise of 11° from −12°C? ________
6. What will the temperature be if there is a rise of 32° from −15°C? ________

Reading and writing large numbers

When you write a number, think about what each digit represents.
Watch out for the zeros.
For nine thousand and six, write 9006. The '9' digit is in the 1000s place, so don't write 90006!

1. Write these amounts in figures.

a. forty-three ______________

b. two hundred and seventy-eight ______________

c. five thousand, nine hundred and sixty-one ______________

d. twenty-one thousand, six hundred and eighty-three ______________

e. four hundred and fifty-seven thousand, nine hundred and thirty-two ______________

f. seven thousand and nineteen ______________

g. ten thousand and two ______________

h. eighty-eight thousand and eight ______________

2. Write these amounts in words.

a. 105 ______________________________

b. 150 ______________________________

c. 8006 ______________________________

d. 8060 ______________________________

e. 8600 ______________________________

f. 6008 ______________________________

Number and place value

Place value in large numbers

When you are working out how many 100s there are in, say, 4516, remember that there are 10 hundreds in 1000. So, 4516 = 45 hundreds + 16.

1. Match the answer to each problem with the same amount in words. The first one has been done for you.

a. 368 + 320 = 688	One thousand and seventy-two
b. 4290 + 14 = ______	Twenty-four thousand, one hundred and fifty
c. 1472 – 400 = ______	Six hundred and eighty-eight
d. 61,300 + 291 = ______	Sixty-one thousand five hundred and ninety-one
e. 25,000 – 850 = ______	Four thousand, three hundred and four

2. Write down the answer in the first box. In the second box, give the value of the 7 in the answer. The first one has been done for you.

a. 384ml – 9ml = [375ml] [70ml]

b. 443cm + 14cm = [ ] [ ]

c. 758mm + 8mm = [ ] [ ]

d. 990cm – 260cm = [ ] [ ]

e. 1.43m + 5.30m = [ ] [ ]

f 7095m + 50m = [ ] [ ]

g. 8020g – 25g = [ ] [ ]

h. £4762 – £8 = [ ] [ ]

3. Give the answers to the following problems in figures.

a. How many tens in three hundred and eighty-seven? ______

b. How many hundreds in twenty-four thousand and fifty-six? ______

c. Which is less: 53 hundreds *or* five thousand, two hundred? ______

Roman numerals

The Romans wrote numbers using letters.

I = 1 V = 5 X = 10 L = 50 C = 100 D = 500 M = 1000

When a letter comes **after** a larger letter it is added:
VI = V + I = 5 + 1 = 6

When a letter comes **before** a larger letter it is subtracted:
IX = X − I = 10 − 1 = 9

VIII is 5 + 1 + 1 + 1 = 8

DL is 500 + 50 = 550

LXIV is 50 + 10 + 4 = 64

DCCCXC is 500 + 100 + 100 + 100 + 90 = 890

1. Work out these Roman numerals.

a. VII = ______________	b. CLIII = ______________
c. XIX = ______________	d. CIX = ______________
e. XXXV = ______________	f. DLI = ______________
g. XXXVIII =______________	h. DCCX = ______________
i. LXX = ______________	j. CCCXX = ______________
k. MCM = ______________	l. MDCLV = ______________

Years in Roman numerals

Years are sometimes written in Roman numerals.
The year 1666 would be MDCLXVI = 1000 + 500 + 100 + 50 + 10 + 5 + 1 = 1666.

Remember:
I = 1 V = 5 X = 10 L = 50 C = 100 D = 500 M = 1000

1. Draw a line to match each date written in Roman numerals to our number system.

MC	1650
MCCC	1100
MDCL	2014
MM	1300
MMXIV	2010
MMX	2000

2. Write the year in which you were born in Roman numerals.

Ordering hundreds and thousands

To order 635, 832, 752, 823, look at the 100s digit first.

635 has the lowest 100s digit, then **7**52. Next, **8**32 and **8**23 both have **8** hundreds; so now look at the 10s digit: 8**2**3 has fewer 10s than 8**3**2. So the correct order is: 635, 752, 823, 852.

1. List all of the numbers you can make using all of the digits given. List them in ascending order, smallest first.

a. 2 8 ____________________

b. 6 7 ____________________

c. 4 5 9 ____________________

d. 6 1 8 ____________________

e. 5 8 7 3 ____________________

f. 7 0 4 3 ____________________

Number and place value

Rounding to the nearest 10 and 100

Remember:

- 5**5** rounded to the nearest 10 is 60. When the 1s digit is 5 or more, round up.
- 8**3** rounded to the nearest 10 is 80. When the 1s digit is less than 5, round down.
- 5**4**6 rounded to the nearest 100 is 500. When the 10s digit is less than 5, round down
- 9**8**2 rounded to the nearest 100 is 1000. When the 10s digit is 5 or more, round up.

1. Search for lines of four numbers that round to the same nearest whole 10 or 100. For example, 16, 18, 19 and 21 all round to 20. Colour or circle the lines of numbers that you find.

16	18	19	21	385
894	141	6	204	401
59	60	61	64	399
112	138	912	249	403
897	913	933	935	226
1001	81	78	77	76
999	206	189	177	179
989	167	888	42	214
1004	188	186	194	187
566	581	612	601	26

Rounding to the nearest 1000, 10,000 and 100,000

To round 167,364 to the nearest 1000 look at the last four digits and round them up or down:
16**7,364** rounds to 167,000 because 7364 is closer to 7000 than 8000.

1. These are the TV viewing figures for a week. Round the figures to the nearest 1000, 10,000 and 100,000. The first one has been done for you.

Programme	Viewers	Rounded to the nearest 1000	Rounded to the nearest 10,000	Rounded to the nearest 100,000
Londoners	178,473	178,000	180,000	200,000
Sing to Win	374,294			
Emergency Ward	472,672			
Football Live	835,333			
The Constabulary	472,567			
All Aboard!	628,342			
Daily News	934,681			
Cooking Today	462,489			
School Quiz Challenge	814,557			
Star Quality	992,103			

2. Roughly how many viewers watched the following programmes? Answer to the nearest 1000.

a. *Londoners* and *Emergency Ward* ________________

b. *The Constabulary* and *Star Quality*________________

c. *Daily News* and *Football Live* ________________

d. *School Quiz Challenge* and *All Aboard!*________________

Number problems (1)

Temperatures below 0°C have a minus sign. To compare temperatures you can use < (less than) and > (greater than). For example, 3 < 6, 6 > 3.

–5 –4 –3 –2 –1 0 1 2 3 4 5

1. Look at the chart below. Write the temperatures in ascending order below.

Temperatures in °C

Amsterdam	13	Dublin	11	London	13	Nairobi	20
Beijing	8	Edinburgh	10	Los Angeles	18	New York	6
Berlin	10	Florence	21	Malta	23	Oslo	4
Cairo	24	Gibraltar	22	Montreal	0	Tel Aviv	25
Cardiff	11	Guernsey	15	Moscow	–2	Toronto	5
Corfu	20	Helsinki	–1	Mumbai	34	Vienna	6

coldest ______________________________

____

____

______________________________ warmest

2. Write four sentences that compare the temperatures in different places. For example, Helsinki is cold but Moscow is slightly colder: –2 < –1. Corfu is cooler than Malta, which is hotter than Vienna: 20 < 23 > 6.

____

____

____

____

Number problems (2)

Remember:

- Numbers get smaller as you count back along the number line, so $-8 < -3$.
- Ascending order means starting with the smallest number.
- Descending order means starting with the largest number.

Use what you know about numbers to answer these questions.

1. The lowest recorded temperatures in six British cities were:
   Belfast –13°C, Birmingham –12°C, Cardiff –9°C, Edinburgh –17°C, London –10°C, Plymouth –8°C. Arrange the cities in ascending order of temperature.

   ____

2. Write these lowest recorded July temperatures in descending order:
   Bombay 22°C, Canberra –10°C, Milan 10°C, Santiago –4°C, Antarctica –36°C, Tokyo 13°C.

   ____

3. The temperature in Kendra's workshop rose 8°C between 9am and 5pm.
   It was 6°C at 5pm. What was the temperature at 9am?

   ____

4. The temperature in the fridge is 3°C. The temperature in the freezer is –18°C.
   How many degrees colder is the freezer?

   ____

Addition and subtraction

Pairs and doubles

Choose the best strategy for adding numbers mentally.
Use number facts that you know, such as doubles and bonds to 10 and 100.

1. Next to each number, write the amount that needs to be added to it to make 50.

a. 24 ______ b. 36 ______ c. 48______ d. 18______

2. Write the amount that needs to be added to these numbers to make 100.

a. 56 ______ b. 73 ______ c. 22 ______ d. 17______

3. Answer the question in the units shown.

a. 260p + 390p = £ _____ b. 740p + 780p = £ _____

c. 910cm + 520cm = _____ m d. 830cm + 320cm = _____ m

e. £2.70 + £9.80 = _____ p f. £8.70 + £4.40 = _____ p

4. Double the first number and then double that answer. There first one has been done for you.

a.

31	62	124
46		
17		
37		
24		
12		

b.

48		
27		
16		
42		
23		
35		

c.

39		
21		
49		
15		
28		
19		

Adding order

When you add numbers in your head it is often easier to start with the largest number. When there are several small numbers, look for pairs that sum to 10.

6 + 6 + 14 + 373 + 4 + 4 = 373 + 14 + 6 + 6 + 4 + 4 = 373 + 20 + 10 + 4 = 407

1. Rearrange these sums in your head so that you start with the largest amount, then write your answer. Look for number bonds.

a. 7 + 8 + 3 + 115 + 2 + 25 = ______

b. 4 + 3 + 14 + 7 + 6 + 506 = ______

c. 22 + 1 + 748 + 9 + 3 + 7 = ______

d. 5 + 6 + 26 + 5 + 4 + 364 = ______

e. 13 + 2 + 1 + 8 + 9 + 727 = ______

f. 6 + 2 + 17 + 243 + 8 + 4 = ______

g. 2 + 4 + 13 + 8 + 6 + 637 = ______

h. 9 + 8 + 1 + 856 + 2 + 24 = ______

2. Answer these questions. Remember the rule about putting the largest number first.

a. The masses of three different crayons are 55g, 65g and 70g. Calculate the total mass of all three crayons. ______

b. Class 1 has seventeen children, Class 2 twenty-four children and Class 3 thirty-six children. Find the number of children in all three classes. ______

3. Write a three-number addition using the numbers below. Put the largest number first. Repeat and use a different set of three numbers for each sum. Now work out your sums.

10	65	11	100	35	15	80	20	30	55	33	85	90
95	66	44	110	110	75	99	40	45	5	77	25	88

______ ______

______ ______

Near doubles and trebles

Looking for doubles can help you calculate additions quickly:

300 + 290 = 590 This sum can be done quickly by saying double 300 minus 10.
450 + 455 = 905 This sum can be done quickly by saying double 450 plus 5.

1. Add these near doubles.

a. 350 + 360 = ☐

b. 600 + 570 = ☐

c. 920 + 900 = ☐

d. 430 + 400 = ☐

e. 200 + 190 + 190 = ☐

f. 100 + 110 + 110 = ☐

g. 300 + 280 + 280 = ☐

h. 199 + 201 + 200 = ☐

i. 790 + 800 = ☐

j. 945 + 950 = ☐

k. 550 + 530 = ☐

l. 250 + 230 = ☐

Here are two other ways to think when adding near doubles (there are also other ways).

690 + 680 = 700 + 700 −10 − 20 = 1370

800 + 800 = 1000 + 1000 − 200 − 200 = 1600

2. Write out your thinking process when you do these sums.

a. £470 + £490 =

____

b. 610m + 620m =

____

Partitioning and recombining

You can split up numbers in a calculation any way you like to help you work out the answer. Remember that you have to put the number back together though!

For example:
234 + 48 = 230 + 40 plus 4 + 8 = 270 + 12 = 282

1. Complete these two calculations. Show your working.

a. 558 + 46 = ______________________

b. 37 + 755 = ______________________

2. Look at the example calculation. Complete a in the same way then answer b by *thinking* in the same way.

427 + 49 = 427 + 3 + 46 = 430 + 46 = 476

a. 642 + 29 = ______________________

b. 876 + 37 = __________ 257 + 28 = __________ 385 + 46 = __________

3. Look at the completed grid below. Read it from left to right and top to bottom as you would a book. Now fill in the other two grids in the same way to find the answers.

	624	+	355		
=	600	+	300		
+	20	+	50		
+	4	+	5		
=	900	+	70	+	9
=	979				

	434	+	242		
=		+			
+		+			
+		+			
=		+		+	
=					

		+			
=	200	+			
+		+	20		
+	4	+			
=		+		+	
=	959				

Bridging and adjusting

Look for numbers that are close to a multiple of 10, so that you can round to a multiple of 10 and then add or subtract a small number (adjusting). For example:

64 + 79 = 143 Work this out as 64 + 80 – 1 = 143

138 – 47 = 91 Work this out as 138 – 50 + 3 = 91

1. Complete these calculations. Show your working.

a. 62 + 56 = ______________________

b. 94 + 87 = ______________________

c. 83 + 78 = ______________________

d. 82 + 99 = ______________________

Here are other ways of thinking when adding and subtracting.

137 + 39 = 137 + 40 – 1 = 176 137 + 41 = 137 + 40 + 1 = 178

187 – 21 = 187 – 20 – 1 = 166 187 – 19 = 187 – 20 + 1 = 168

2. Now do these problems in the same way, showing your working.

a.	157	+	19	=	157 + 20 – 1	=	176
b.	385	–	69	=		=	
c.	537	+	41	=		=	
d.	542	–	21	=		=	
e.	246	+	39	=		=	

3. Solve this problem using one of the strategies suggested on this page.

A jar contained 454g of marmalade. Seventy-nine grams of the marmalade were eaten.

What mass still remained in the jar? ______________________

Mental addition and subtraction

Choose the best strategy for the numbers in the questions.

Counting up and bridging through tens or hundreds is useful for mental subtraction.

Partition the numbers to make them easier to add or subtract mentally.

Work out the answers to these problems. Think carefully about which strategy you are going to use.

1. £370.00 + £250.00 = ____________________

2. 920km take away 480km = ____________________

3. 3687 miles – 800 miles = ____________________

4. 900kg + 726kg = ____________________

5. 740g minus 360g = ____________________

6. 982 litres + 600 litres = ____________________

7. From 3000m take away four hundred and seven hundred metres.

   ____

8. A train travels 700km, 400km and 900km. How far is that?

   ____

Addition and subtraction

Written addition and subtraction

Practise your skills in column addition and subtraction.

```
  7885        6 12 1
+ 6422        7 3 2 9
 14307      - 4 5 7 1
   1 1        2 7 5 8
```

Work out these problems using a written calculation method.

a.	4210 + 6709	
b.	2708 + 307	
c.	1143 + 115	
d.	349 – 164	
e.	8302 – 3408	
f.	8707 – 2819	
g.	4369 + 7098	

Add it!

You can use column addition and subtraction for numbers with more than four digits. Line up the digits and check your working carefully!

```
  37691
+ 66081
 103772
  1  1
```

1. Use the written vertical method of addition that you have learned to do these calculations.

a. 57480 + 60926	b. 10245 + 92
c. 67553 + 11101	d. 50748 + 66092
e. 87486 + 10323	f. 90067 + 33908

2. Set these questions out in columns, then work them out.

a. 52350 + 40031	b. 63174 + 80921

Addition and subtraction

Take it away!

If there is a zero in the top row, remember to exchange from the next column. Don't subtract the top digit from the bottom one! For example, work out 2340 – 1628 like this:

```
  2340          ¹ ¹ ³ ¹
- 1628          2̸ 3 4̸ 0
                -1 6 2 8
                   7 1 2
```

1. Use the written vertical method of subtraction that you have learned at school to do these calculations.

a. 570 – 332 = ______

b. 827 – 414 = ______

c. 2461 – 1347 = ______

d. 3514 – 1367 = ______

e. 892 – 423 = ______

f.
```
  3509
  2750
  ____
```

2. An outward flight to America carries 427 people and the return flight carries 579 people.

a. What is the total number of people carried on the two flights?

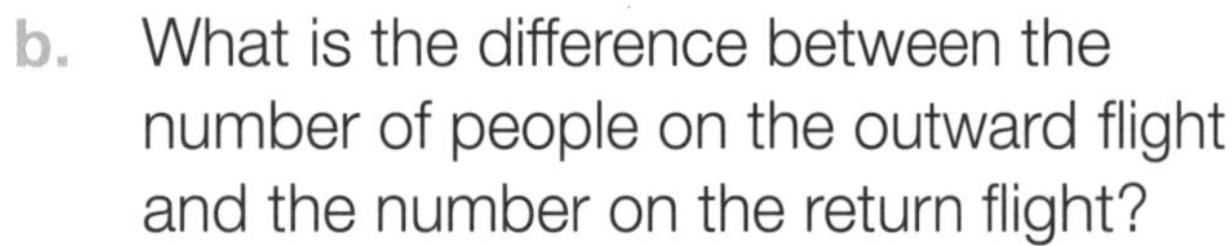

b. What is the difference between the number of people on the outward flight and the number on the return flight?

Adding and subtracting practice (1)

Set the numbers out carefully when you write the questions in columns. If there is a different number of digits in the two numbers, make sure that the digits are lined up correctly.
For example:

```
  1833          1833
+  254   not   +254
 _____          _____
```

1. Use the column method of adding and subtracting to answer these questions.

a. 1933 + 364	b. 1382 – 242
c. 1844 + 2936	d. 2936 – 1749
e. £38.96 + £65.05	f. £390.84 – £127.58

g. Jane saved £71.83 and earned £28.55 more. How much money does she have altogether?

h. Ali has a collection of 1043 game cards. He gives away 168 of them. How many does he have left?

Adding and subtracting practice (2)

When you are adding money, make sure that you use the pound sign and make sure the decimal points are lined up in the correct place.

```
  £20.25
+ £17.92
  £38.17
    1
```

1. Use column addition or subtraction to solve the following questions.

a. £30.14 + £18.96 =	b. 1143 – 120 =
c. £39.25 – £12.56 =	d. My cat weighs 3.4kg and my dog weighs 12.52kg. How much is their combined mass?
e. Two numbers have a difference of 1.56. One of the numbers is 7.92. What is the other number? Can there be more than one answer? Why?	f. I buy some jeans costing £29.54 and a scarf costing £3.98. I pay with two £20 notes and receive change of £16.48. Is this correct?

Adding and subtracting practice (3)

Remember that you can use what you know about inverses to answer some questions, because addition is the inverse of subtraction. For example:

[ ] + £36.37 = £38.00

£38.00 – £36.37 = £1.63

so **£1.63** + £36.37 = £38.00

1. Use column addition or subtraction to solve the following questions.

a. 32,668 + 14,825 =	b. £31.17 + £17.92 =
c. 13,057 – 12,436 =	d. £58.25 – £23.72 =
e. Fill in the blank: [ ] – 3.40 = 21.70	f. Fill in the blank: 72.90 – [ ] = 49.70
g. Two numbers have a difference of 2.72. One of the numbers is 6.81. What is the other number? Can there be more than one answer? Why?	h. In a sponsored event, Tracy raised £36.80, Alesha raised £29.00 and Andy raised £15.55. How much did the three friends raise altogether?

Spot the deliberate mistake

Check that the numbers in the questions are set out correctly.
Put tenths under tenths, ones under ones, tens under tens, hundreds under hundreds, and so on. It might help if you estimate the answers before you work them out.

1. Each of these calculations has mistakes. Rewrite and solve them correctly.

a. 24.3 + 12.62

```
   24.3
+ 12.62
  150.5
```

b. 899 – 67.4

```
   899
– 67.4
   225
```

c. 9 – 7.2

```
  8 1
  9.00
– 7.20
  1.10
```

You're the teacher

Take care when you write the numbers in each question in columns.
Check that you have written each number or amount correctly before you do the calculation.

1. Here is a copy of Mike's test paper. Use column addition to check each answer. Use the space on the right to show your working. Tick the correct answers and write the correct answers for the ones he got wrong.

Mike Jones **12 May 2014**

1. £1.45 + £1.78 + £2.43 = £5.73

2. £2.99 + £4.28 + 68p = £7.97

3. £2.37 + £8.25 + £1.12 = £11.74

4. £7.70 + £7.07 + 70p = £21.77

5. 98p + £3.69 + £6.16 + 46p = £11.26

6. £16.72 + £56.88 + £31.99 = £104.60

How many questions did Mike answer correctly? ____________________

Round, estimate, check

You can use rounding to help estimate an answer before you do the calculation.

For example, to work out 5002 + 4142.
Estimate: 5000 + 4100 = 9100.

1. Round these numbers then estimate the answer. Calculate the answer using the most efficient and appropriate method. Then check your answer by doing an inverse calculation.

a. 2005 + 3290

Answer: ________

b. 5002 – 1386

Answer: ________

c. 7211 – 2595

Answer: ________

d. 2734 + 1992

Answer: ________

e. 9018 – 8933

Answer: ________

Estimate and win!

You can use what you know about inverses to help find missing digits:
57 + 5 □ 4 = 601. To find the missing digit, subtract 57 from 601. 601 − 57 = 544.

1. For these questions, round the numbers and estimate the answer. Look at your estimate to check that your answer is likely to be correct. Then use a written method to work out the answers.

a. 362 + 145
Estimate ______________________
____

b. £53.59 + £188.24
Estimate ______________________
____

c. 748 – 226
Estimate ______________________
____

d. 58.43m – 27.7m
Estimate ______________________
____

2. Fill in the missing numbers in these calculations.

a.
```
   □ 5 7
 + 2 □ 3
 -------
   6 6 0
```

b.
```
   8 □ 6 7
 − 1 3 □ 4
 ---------
   6 8 1 3
```

c.
```
  £ □ 9 5 □
− £ 3 1 □ 6
-----------
  £ 5 8 2 4
```

Using multiplication facts

Remember your multiplication facts, and use them to help you.

For 6, 5 and 30 you know that 6 × 5 = 30 and 5 × 6 = 30. So 30 ÷ 5 = 6 and 30 ÷ 6 = 5.

1. For each trio of numbers, write four number sentences.

a. 6 4 24 ______ ______ ______ ______

b. 3 18 6 ______ ______ ______ ______

c. 5 8 40 ______ ______ ______ ______

d. 7 8 56 ______ ______ ______ ______

2. Write as many multiplication and division sentences as you can for the following numbers.

a. 48 ______

______

______

b. 320 ______

______

______

3. Look at this list and circle the three numbers that have a remainder of 2 when divided by 5.

27 25 21 32 16 47 19 23 41

Multiples

A multiple is what you get when you multiply a number by another whole number.
35 is a multiple of 5 and 7 because 5 × 7 = 35.
5 and 7 are factors of 35.

Look at each number. For each one, write as many multiplication facts as you can. The first one is done for you.

2 × 6 = 12

12 — 3 × 4 = 12

1 × 12 = 12

12	81	30	48
72	32	49	42
21	35	18	36
56	64	63	27
40	90	28	16

Know your multiples

Remember what you know about multiples.

For example, multiples of 6 are divisible by 2 and 3.

1. **Colour all the multiples of:**
   - **6 red**
   - **7 blue**
   - **8 yellow**
   - **9 purple**
   - **10 orange.**

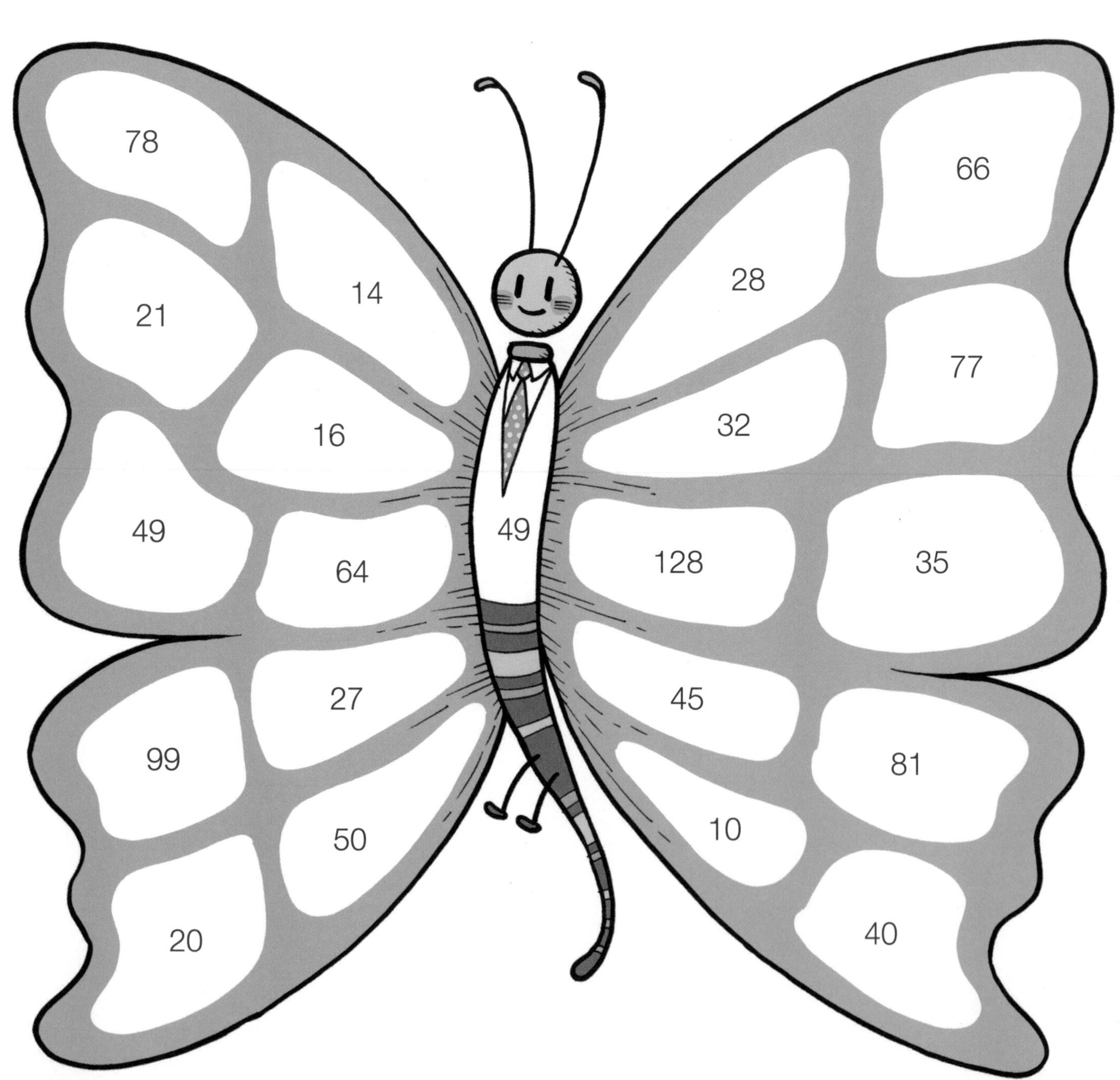

Times-tables builder

You can work out new facts by using facts that you already know and using patterns.

1. Complete these times tables. You should know these already.

10×	3×	4×
1 × 10 = 10	1 × 3 = 3	1 × 4 = 4
2 × 10 =	2 × 3 =	2 × 4 =
3 × 10 =	3 × 3 =	3 × 4 =
4 × 10 =	4 × 3 =	4 × 4 =
5 × 10 =	5 × 3 =	5 × 4 =
6 × 10 =	6 × 3 =	6 × 4 =
7 × 10 =	7 × 3 =	7 × 4 =
8 × 10 =	8 × 3 =	8 × 4 =
9 × 10 =	9 × 3 =	9 × 4 =
10 × 10 =	10 × 3 =	10 × 4 =
11 × 10 =	11 × 3 =	11 × 4 =
12 × 10 =	12 × 3 =	12 × 4 =

2. Use the 10-, 3- and 4-times tables to build up the following times tables.

13× = 10× + 3×		14× = 10× + 4×	
1 × 13 =	2 × 13 =	1 × 14 =	2 × 14 =
3 × 13 =	4 × 13 =	3 × 14 =	4 × 14 =
5 × 13 =	6 × 13 =	5 × 14 =	6 × 14 =
7 × 13 =	8 × 13 =	7 × 14 =	8 × 14 =
9 × 13 =	10 × 13 =	9 × 14 =	10 × 14 =
11 × 13 =	12 × 13 =	11 × 14 =	12 × 14 =

Divisibility tests

'Divisible by' means *when you divide one number by another, the result is a whole number.* When a number is divisible by another number, then it is also divisible by each of the factors of that number. So if a number is divisible by 6, it is also divisible by 2 and 3. Remember:

- Multiples of 2 are even.
- Multiples of 3 have a digit sum that is also a multiple of 3.
- Multiples of 4 can be halved to give an even number.
- Multiples of 5 end in 0 or 5.
- Multiples of 6 are even multiples of 3.
- Multiples of 9 have a digit sum that is also a multiple of 9.

1. Use the above rules to check the following numbers. The first one has been done for you.

a. 144 is a multiple of 2, 3, 4 and 6.

b. 225 is a multiple of ______________________

c. 390 is a multiple of ______________________

d. 960 is a multiple of ______________________

2. Multiples of 4 can be halved to give an even number. Extend this idea and invent a rule to test for multiples of 8. Show your method works with some examples.

____

____

____

3. Find the smallest number that is a multiple of all of 2, 3, 4, 5, 6, 8 and 9.

____

Factor trees

Factor trees are drawn by splitting up numbers into multiplication facts. For example, the factors of 18 are 1, 2, 3, 6, 9 and 18.

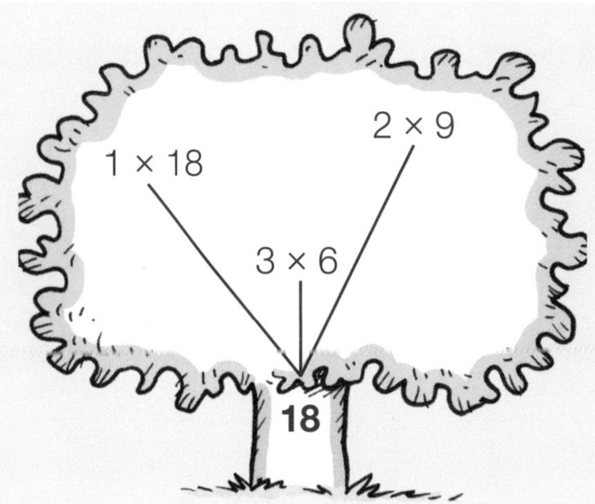

Work systematically when you are finding multiplication facts. Use what you know about other numbers to help you. For example, use what you know about multiplication facts for 18 to help you find them for 36.

1. Use the drawings below to make factor trees for the following numbers.

a. 24

b. 28

c. 36

d. 40

e. 64

f. 85

Identify common factors

It helps to look at the largest factors first when you are trying to find a range of common factors.

1. Femi says that he has found all of the factors for 32, the age of his dad. He found four factors. Femi's dad says he is wrong and that there are five factors. Can you find the correct answer?

2. Answer these questions.

a. Find a 2-digit number that has 1, 2, 3, 4, 5 and 6 as factors.

b. Explain why there is only one 2-digit number with this property.

Using factors to solve problems

You can use factors to solve problems. If you find more than one combination of factors, then solve the problem using the ones you find easiest to calculate. Remember, there may be more than one combination of factors you could try! For example:

$$12 \times 20 =$$
$$(6 \times 2) \times (2 \times 10) =$$
$$(2 \times 2) \times 6) \times 10 =$$
$$(4 \times 6) \times 10 =$$
$$24 \times 10 = 240$$

Use factors to solve the following problems.

a. 12 × 18	b. 20 × 17
c. 24 × 15	d. 25 × 24

Prime numbers and composite numbers

Composite numbers have more than two factors.
Prime numbers have only two factors, 1 and themselves.

1. Follow the rules to find the prime numbers up to 100. Work systematically.

1. Shade the number 1, as it is not a prime number.
2. Now choose a new colour for shading.
3. Find the first unshaded square.
4. Leave it unshaded, but shade all of its multiples lightly.
5. Return to rule 2 and repeat the process.

1	2	3	4	5	6	7	8	9	10
11	12	13	14	15	16	17	18	19	20
21	22	23	24	25	26	27	28	29	30
31	32	33	34	35	36	37	38	39	40
41	42	43	44	45	46	47	48	49	50
51	52	53	54	55	56	57	58	59	60
61	62	63	64	65	66	67	68	69	70
71	72	73	74	75	76	77	78	79	80
81	82	83	84	85	86	87	88	89	90
91	92	93	94	95	96	97	98	99	100

2. List all the prime numbers up to 100 here.

Prime factors

Here is a factor tree for the number 42.
To make it we need two numbers that multiply to make 42. We have chosen 6 × 7.

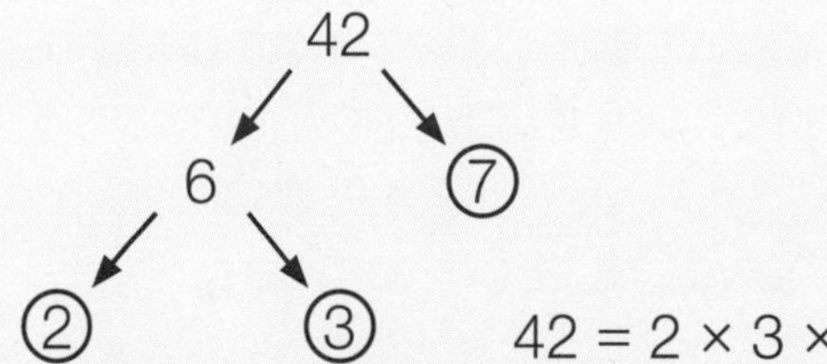

- If a number in the tree is prime put a ring around it.

$42 = 2 \times 3 \times 7$

- If it is not prime, continue by finding two more numbers that you can multiply to make that number. Continue until all numbers are prime. The number at the top is the product of all the prime numbers with rings around them.

1. Make factor trees for 24, 56, 100 and 81. Write each number as the product of its prime factors. The factor tree for 24 has been started for you.

24	56
100	81

2. Form a factor tree for the number 210 and say what is special about the numbers in the tree.

Multiplication and division

Calculation patterns (multiplication and division)

Knowing times-tables facts can help you work out other multiplication and division facts. For example, if you know that 6 × 1 = 6 and 6 × 2 = 12, you also know that 60 × 1 = 60 and 60 × 2 = 120. Knowing doubles and halves of small numbers can help you work out doubles and halves of large numbers.

1. Fill in the numbers in these multiplication patterns.

40	80	120						360	
80		240			480	560			
30				150	180				
60							480		600
50		150	200					450	
100	200					700	800		

2. Use the table to complete these sentences.

a. To find the answers to the 50-times table, multiply by ________ and then halve.

b. The answers to the 30-times table facts are half those of the ________-times table facts.

c. To multiply by ________, multiply by 100 and then double.

d. The answers to the ________-times table facts are half those of the 80-times table facts.

e. To find the ________-times table facts, double the 40-times table facts.

3. Try to work out the pattern of numbers in these halving chains.

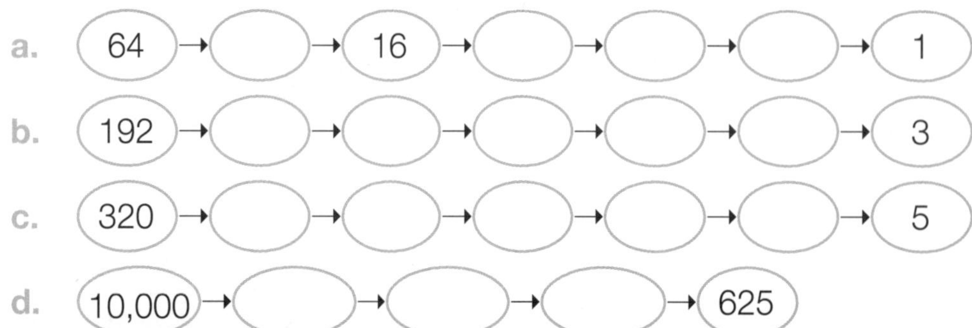

Using related multiplication and division facts

You can work out new facts by:
- using facts that you already know
- using halving or doubling
- using inverse operations.

For example, difficult maths problems can be made easier by doubling one number in the calculation and then halving the result. To solve 16 × 5, 16 × 10 = 160, then 160 ÷ 2 = 80.

Another way to do more difficult multiplications is to halve one number and then double the result. For 20 × 15, 10 × 15 = 150, then 150 × 2 = 300.

1. Solve these problems by doubling a number first, then halving the result.

a. 4 × 45 = ______________________

b. 25 × 8 = ______________________

c. 6 × 45 = ______________________

d. 15 × 8 = ______________________

e. 35 × 9 = ______________________

f. 7 × 15 = ______________________

g. 25 × 9 = ______________________

h. 7 × 55 = ______________________

2. Solve these problems by halving a number first, then doubling the result.

a. 15 × 12 = ______________________

b. 25 × 16 = ______________________

c. 20 × 14 = ______________________

d. 21 × 16 = ______________________

3. Solve these problems mentally by first multiplying by 100 and then halving the result.

a.	74 × 50	=	7400	÷	2	=	3700
c.	38 × 50	=		÷	2	=	
e.	56 × 50	=		÷	2	=	

b.	63 × 50	=	6300	÷	2	=	3150
d.	89 × 50	=		÷	2	=	
f.	45 × 50	=		÷	2	=	

Multiplication and division

Partitioning when multiplying mentally

You can use partitioning to help you with mental calculations.
For example: 43 × 7 = (40 × 7) + (3 × 7) = 280 + 21 = 301

1. Solve these problems. Write out all the thinking stages in the same way as the example above.

a. 96 × 5 = ______________________

b. 8 × 58 ______________________

c. 83 × 6 = ______________________

d. 9 × 74 = ______________________

2. Use the same method to work out the answers to the following.

a.	2	×	64cm	=	128cm
b.	56m	×	7	=	
c.	9	×	37km	=	
d.	79g	×	5	=	
e.	43ml	×	8	=	
f.	5	×	£47	=	
g.	98mm	×	3	=	
h.	6	×	61kg	=	

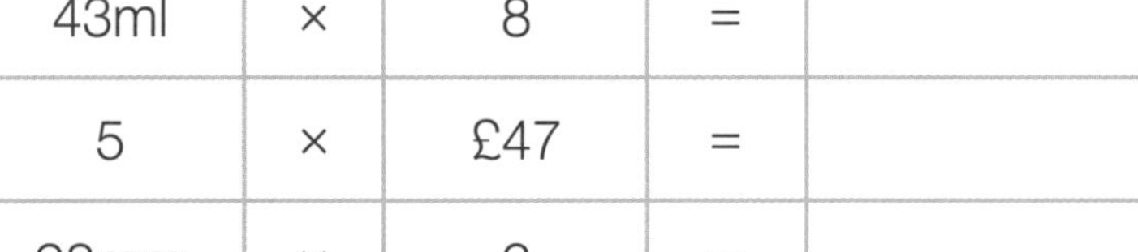

i. What is the cost of five items at 68p each? ______________________

j. Bread is priced at £0.94 per loaf. Find the cost of three loaves. ______________________

k. If a train averages 57mph how far will it travel in 3 hours? ______________________

Division with remainders

When you divide, estimate the answer first.
Split up the number you are dividing to make it easy to divide.

1. Fill in these division charts using mental methods. Write the answer with the remainder. The first one has been done for you.

	÷	26	53	64	107
a.	5	5			
	r	1			
b.	7				
	r				

	÷	29	40	79	113
c.	3				
	r				
d.	9				
	r				

2. Read these questions carefully and then work out the answers.

a. There are 47 children on a trip.

How many groups of three children can be made? ________________

How many children will be left over? ________________

b. How many packets of biscuits can be brought with £10.00

if each packet costs £0.90? ________________

What amount of money will be left

over? ________________

Written multiplication strategies

Here is a reminder of the written column method of short multiplication. Remember to line the digits up correctly.

```
  1 4 2
×     7
-------
  9 9 4
  2 1
```

1. Answer these multiplication questions using a written column method.

a. 136 × 4	b. 214 × 6
c. 45 × 8	d. 54 × 7
e. There were 28 rows of 9 chairs in a school hall. How many people could be seated altogether?	f. Cara collected 115 sets of animal stickers. There were 5 stickers in each set. How many individual stickers has she collected?

Written multiplication practice

Here is a reminder of the written column method for larger numbers (long multiplication):

```
  2 4
× 1 6
2 4 0  First multiply 24 × 10
1 4 4  Then multiply 24 × 6
3 8 4  Then add to find the total.
```

1. Answer these multiplication questions using the written column method.

a. 318 × 6	b. 256 × 5	c. 26 × 32
d. 77 × 21	e. 8525 × 7	f. 7348 × 29

Divided up

Here is a simple division for 105 ÷ 7 using a written method. As with all written calculations, keep all the columns lined up at all times.

$\begin{array}{r} 1\ 5 \\ 7 \overline{)\ 1\ 0\ {}^{3}5} \end{array}$ Answer: 15	7 goes into 10 once, with 3 left over. The 1 is written in the 10s column and the 3 is carried over to the 1s joining with the 5 to make 35. 7 goes into 35 five times with no remainder. The 5 is written in the 1s column.

1. Use the written method of division above to work these out.

a. $6 \overline{)\ 1\ 5\ 6}$	b. $5 \overline{)\ 9\ 5\ 5}$
c. Set this question out yourself. 560 ÷ 4	d. Set this question out yourself. 900 ÷ 6
e. There are 52 children at a party. They need teams of 4 for a game. How many teams can they make?	f. There are 92 balloons in a box. There are four colours of balloon. There is the same number of each colour. How many of each colour are there?

Written division (with remainders)

Here is a simple division for 437 ÷ 5 using a written method:

```
   8 7 r 2
5 | 4 3 ³7
```

Answer: 87 remainder 2

5 goes into 43 eight times with 3 left over.
The 8 is written in the 10s column and the 3 is carried over to the 1s joining with the 7 to make 37.
5 goes into 37 seven times with 2 left over. The 7 is written in the 1s column and we write the remainder as r2.

1. Use a written method to solve these divisions. Remember to write the remainder clearly.

a.	b.
4 | 2 6 7	5 | 4 1 7
c.	**d.**
4 | 1 4 5	4 | 6 2 5
e.	**f.**
5 | 1 6 7	8 | 1 0 7 9

Multiplication and division

Multiplying and dividing by 10, 100 and 1000

When you **multiply** a number by **100**, its digits move **2 places to the left**: 54 × 100 = 5400.

When you **multiply** a number by **1000**, its digits move **3 places to the left**: 54 × 1000 = 54,000.

When you **divide** a number by **100**, its digits move **2 places to the right**: 23,000 ÷ 100 = 230.

When you **divide** a number by **1000**, its digits move **3 places to the right**: 23,000 ÷ 1000 = 23.

1. Make each amount 10, 100 and 1000 times larger.

		× 10	× 100	× 1000
a.	£35		£3500	
b.	12.5m			12,500m
c.	$6\frac{1}{2}$km			
d.	3.45g		345g	
e.	$6\frac{1}{4}$kg			6250kg
f.	4.02g		402g	
g.	$6\frac{3}{4}$m	67.5m		
h.	£0.05			£50.00
i.	0.020g		2g	
j.	$2\frac{1}{2}$km			2500km

2. Underneath each abacus, write in figures the number that is 10 times smaller than the amount shown.

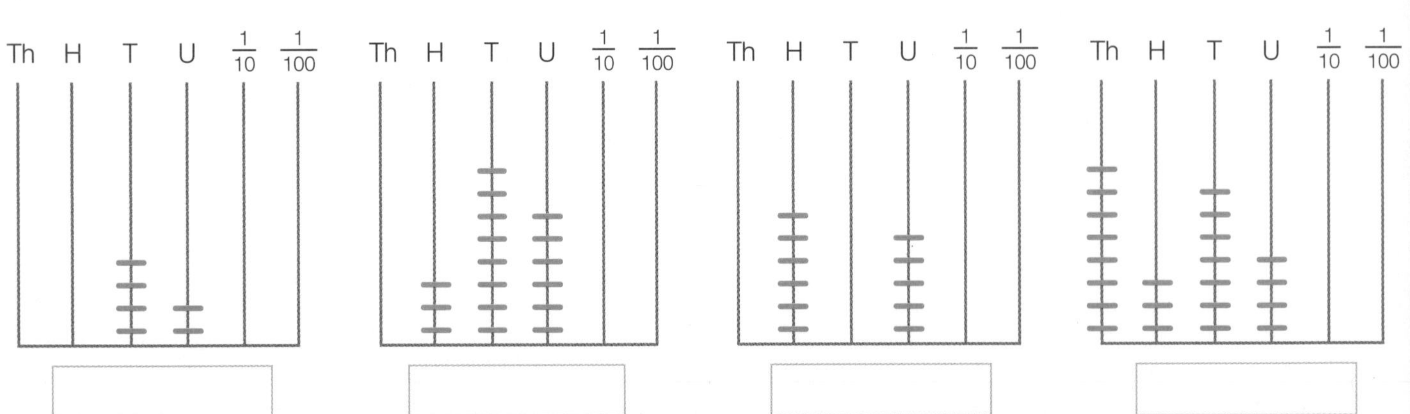

3. **Now, on the abacuses below, show the number that is 10 times smaller again than the figure you have just written.**

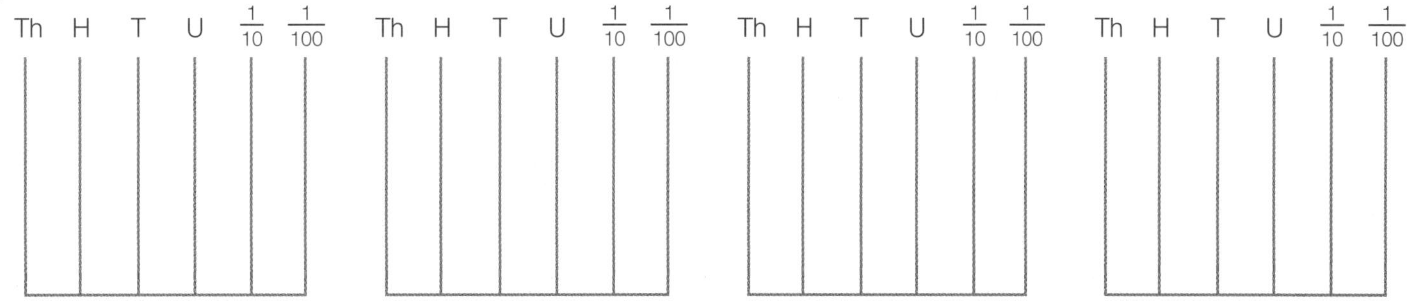

4. **Work out these lengths in millimetres, then change the answers first into centimetres and then into metres as shown.**

a. 620mm × 2 = | 1240mm | 124cm | 1.24m |

b. 6840mm ÷ 2 = | | | |

c. 2 × 805mm = | | | |

d. 2440mm ÷ 4 = | | | |

5. **Answer these problems carefully.**

a. How many times smaller is 32 than three thousand two hundred? ______________

b. Nine pence multiplied by five is ______________ times smaller than £4.50.

c. Plastic cups cost £2.50 per 100. Work out the price of 10 cups.

d. How many times smaller is fifty-six than 5600? ______________

e. 45,000m is the same distance as ______________ kilometres.

Square numbers

A number multiplied by itself makes a square number. 49 is a square number; it can be written as 7 × 7 or 7^2. All square numbers make a square pattern of squares.

1. Complete this square number pattern up to 10 × 10.

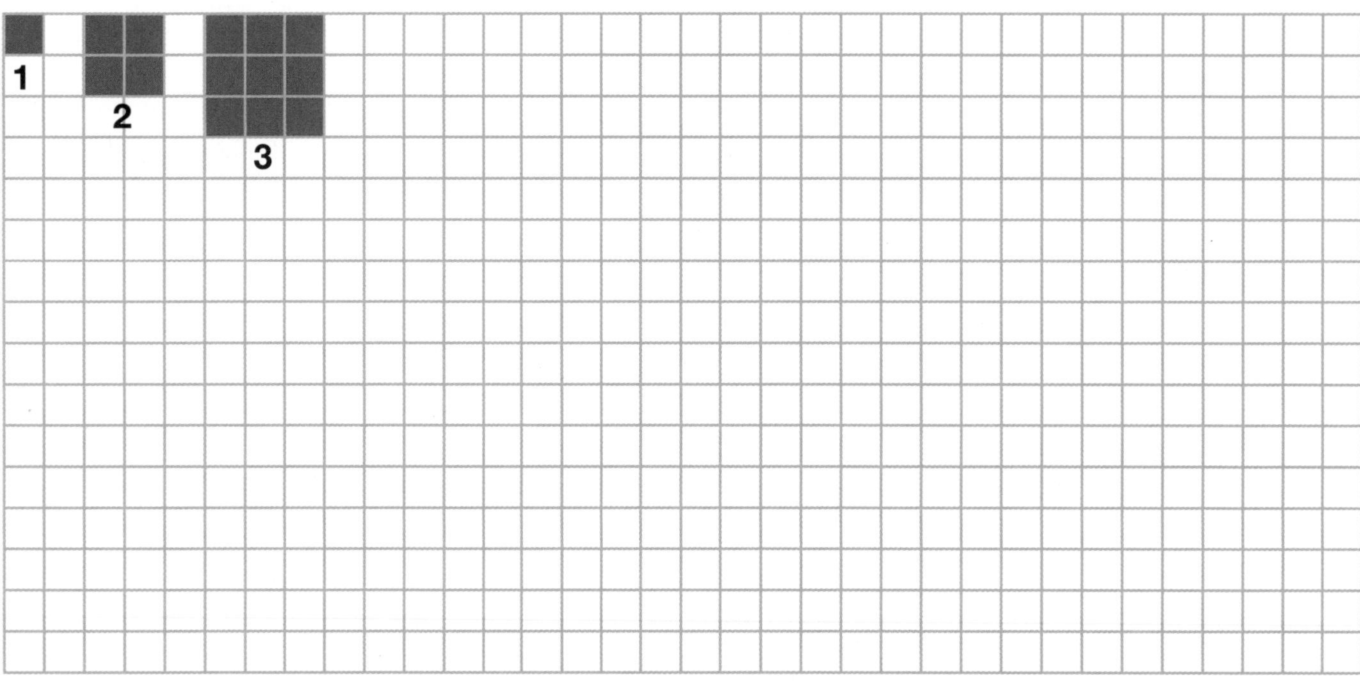

2. Write out the sequence of square numbers and explore the pattern of differences between these numbers.

3. Can you see a relationship? If so, explain what it is. Say how it develops and why.

Square numbers and notation

1. Find a number in a square that is equivalent to each number in a circle. For example, $10^2 = 10 \times 10 = 100$. Join each pair with a line. **Tip:** think about what the final digit will be when a number is squared when you are choosing numbers.

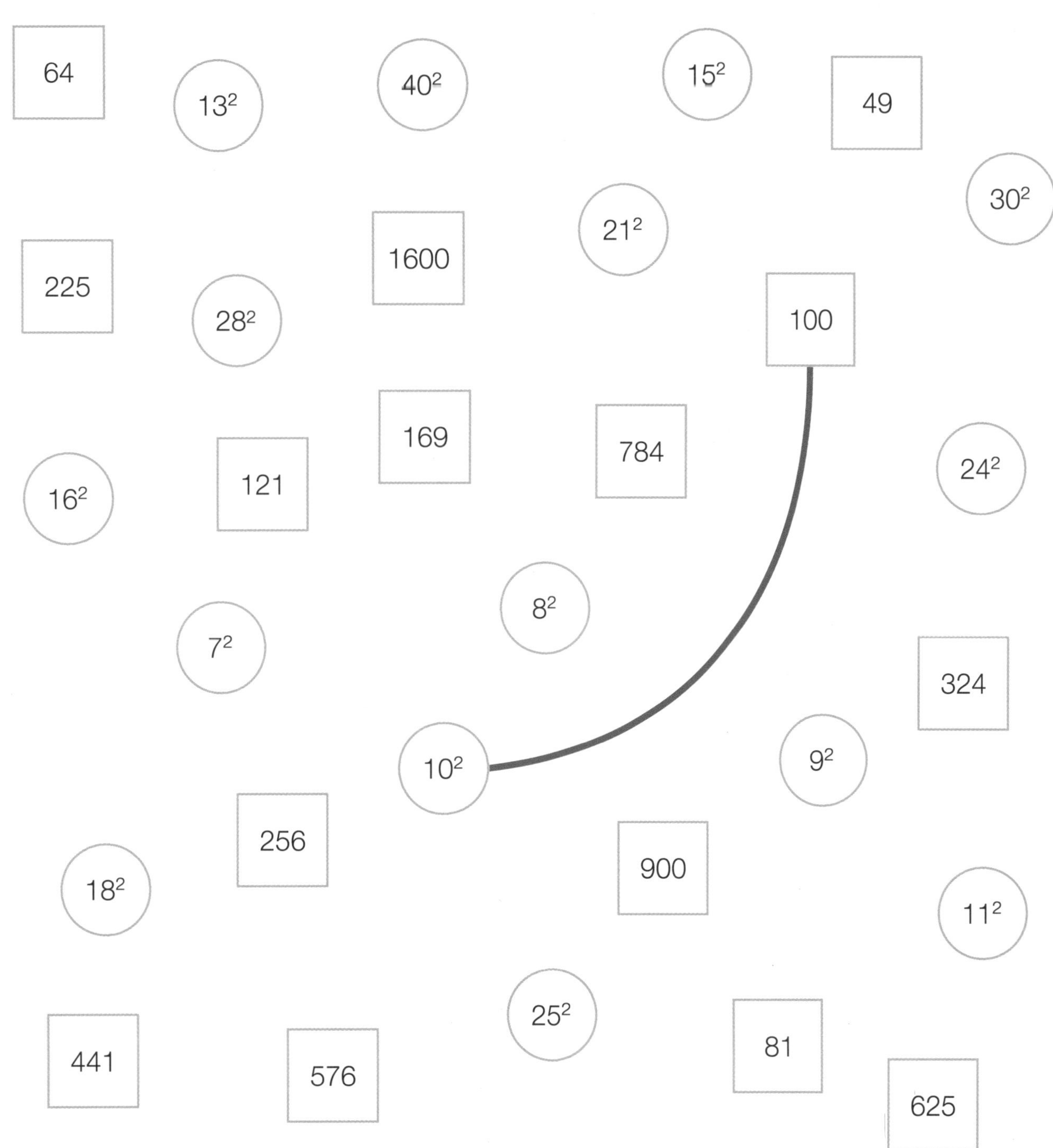

Cube numbers

The cube of a number is a number multiplied by itself twice.
27 is 3^3: $3 \times 3 \times 3 = 27$.

We call the number *three cubed* or *three to the power of three.*

1. Work out the value of these cube numbers. Use the space in each box for your working out.

a. 5^3 = ______________________ = ______________________

b. 4^3 = ______________________ = ______________________

c. 1^3 = ______________________ = ______________________

d. 10^3 = ______________________ = ______________________

e. 7^3 = ______________________ = ______________________

Cube numbers and notation

$8 = 2^3$ because $2 \times 2 \times 2 = 8$.
The *index number* or *power* ^{3} tells you how many times the number is multiplied by itself.

1. Find four more cube numbers and write them as the example below shows.

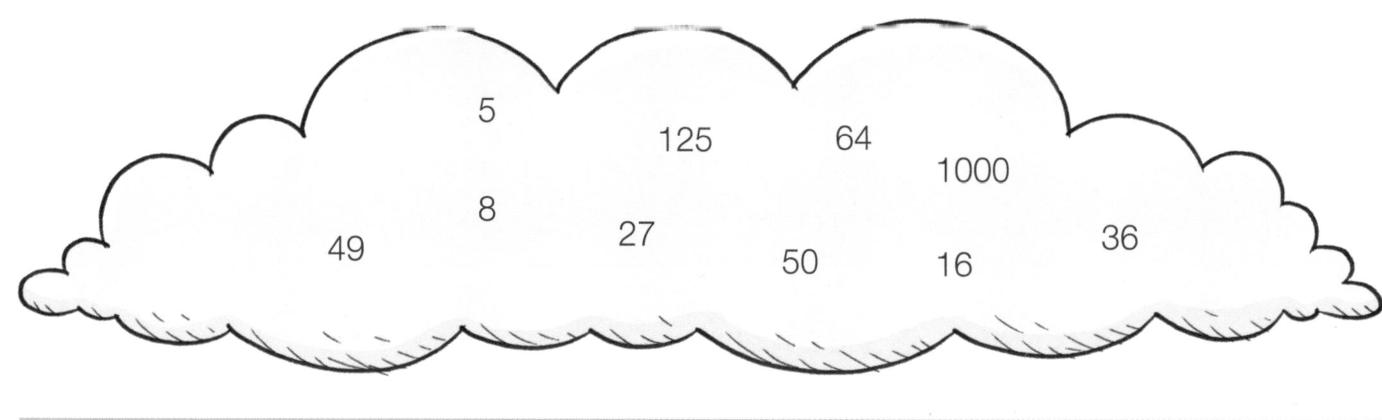

$1 = 1^3$				

2. Work out these cube number problems.

a. Double me is 2^3. What number am I?

____

b. A third of me is 1^3. What number am I?

____

c. I am two more than 3^3.

____

Problem solver

When you are working out a word problem, you need to decide on a sensible way to answer it before you start.
You might use different addition or subtraction methods depending on the numbers in the question.

Complete these questions using the strategies that you have been learning. Show the calculations where necessary.

1. My cat weighs 2.7kg and my dog weighs 11.51kg. How much is their combined mass?

2. Find two numbers between 5 and 6 that total 11.42.

3. Jennie has to download some photos from various memory cards. She has 207 photos on one card and 865 on another.

   a. How many photos has she taken?

   b. She decides that there are 388 photos that she does not want to keep. How many is she going to store?

4. Mr Green has saved £1038 in his bank account. He buys a new television for £659.50. How much does he have left?

5. I buy a shirt costing £12.99 and a pair of jeans costing £21.50. I pay with two £20 notes and receive change of £15.51. Is this correct?

History trip

When you use a written method to solve money problems, make sure that the pounds, the pence and the decimal point line up under each other correctly in columns.

```
    £1.76
×       8
   £14.08
     6 4
```

Class 5B are studying the Romans and go on a trip to a 'Roman Experience' theme park.

There are 31 children in the class. Using the price list, answer the questions below.

Visitors' centre	£1.50
Be a Roman soldier	£1.85
Row the boats as slaves	£0.90
Taste of Ancient Rome	£1.00

1. How much would it cost for class 5B to go just to the visitors' centre?

The children were invited to choose an additional activity. Twelve chose to be a soldier, ten chose to be slaves, and the rest wanted to taste the Roman food.

2. Calculate how much it would cost for each group to go to the visitors' centre **and** to do their chosen activity.

3. If the bus hire costs £54, how much did the whole trip cost?

Restaurant rip-off

This is a bill for a group of seven people who ate at The Fat Goose restaurant. The waiter calculated it incorrectly! Can you spot the mistakes and calculate it correctly? When you solve multi-step problems like these, think carefully about which method to use. Keep track of all the steps as you work out the answer.

The Fat Goose

7 × cocktails @ £3.50 = £25

6 × mineral water @ £1.75 = £10.50

1 × fruit juice @ £1.90 = 90p

5 × set menu @ £23.99 = £112.95

2 × set menu @ £15.95 = £31.80

2 × wine @ £14.65 = £29.30

Service @ £22.95

Total = £250

1. What is the correct total for the bill?

2. Once the waiter has corrected the bill, four of the people decide to split it equally. How much do they pay each?

Operation calculate

1. Cali has a collection of 186 toy farm animals which she no longer plays with. She decides to share them between her 3 young cousins. How many toys do they receive each?

____

2. Jay collects stick insects. They are an average of 7.2cm long. He tells his friend that, if laid end to end, all 9 of them would measure nearly a metre long. Is he correct? What would they actually measure? How close is he?

____

____

3. Felt-tipped pens are sold in packs of 10. Mrs Jones receives 480 pens.

   a. How many packs is that? _______________

   b. There are 6 classes. If she shares the pens equally, how many felt-tipped pens will each class receive? _______________

4. a. There are 432 chairs in the hall. They need to be put around tables in groups of 8. How many table groups will there be?

   ____

   b. Each table needs 3.5 litres of juice. How much juice is needed altogether?

   ____

5. a. There are 824 wheels in a car park. There are only cars parked there. How many cars is that?

   ____

   b. Each driver paid £2.20 to park there. How much money was collected?

   ____

All at sea!

Remember, you can check your answer to a problem by using an inverse operation.

Captain Jack is loading up his ship with supplies for a long voyage. He needs to know how many items he is taking. However, he is not very good at maths! Help him by answering these questions.

1. Captain Jack wants to take 350 nails for each of his three masts. How many nails does he need to bring?

   ____

2. There are eight crew members. Each can bring 256 of their favourite biscuits. How many biscuits can be loaded on board?

   ____

3. Six barrels of apples, each containing 425 apples, are brought below deck. How many apples are there in total?

   ____

4. Each of the eight crew, plus Captain Jack, is allowed 512 rations of their favourite tipple – prune juice. How many rations of prune juice do they bring to drink?

   ____

5. There are seven cannonball racks, each holding 156 cannonballs. How many cannonballs are there in total?

   ____

6. The crew take five parrots and 673 packets of bird seed for each parrot. How many packets of bird seed are packed for the voyage?

   ____

Lots of division

Solve these problems mentally. If you can't do them in your head, use short division to find the answers.

1. Harry has received equal numbers of postcards from 8 different countries. He has received 176 postcards. How many come from each country?

Answer: ______________________

2. a. At the zoo, Tariq saw a number of four-legged animals. They had 312 legs between them. He challenged his sister to work out how many animals he had seen that day.

Answer: ______________________

b. Tariq's sister returned the challenge by saying 'If there were 346 visitors and 24 keepers, how many pairs of shoes were there in the zoo that day?'

Answer: ______________________

3. A baker packs his cakes into boxes of 6 for the supermarket. He has 255 cakes. How many boxes does he make up? Are there any cakes left for his tea?

Answer: ______________________

Calculation problems

Half a bus

For some problems that have a remainder in the answer, you may need to decide whether to round the answer up or down so it makes sense. For example:

There are 16 friends leaving a concert. Five people can fit in a taxi. How many taxis will they need to get home? The answer is four taxis, as three would not be enough. 5 × 3 = 15 and another taxi is needed for the sixteenth person.

Answer these questions. You will need to adjust some of your answers so that they make sense in 'real life'.

1. 216 children are going on a trip. 49 children can fit onto one bus. How many buses need to be hired?

   ____

2. Vicky has to buy 3 lengths of curtain material for her window, each measuring 1.8m. How much does she need to buy altogether?

   ____

3. 129 eggs are packed into boxes of 6. How many boxes are needed?

   ____

4. A sponsored walk is organised so that it is done in 9 laps, to give walkers a rest. Each lap is 3.4km long. How far do the walkers walk in total?

   ____

5. Each jug holds 2.3 litres of water. I fill 7 jugs. How much water have I measured?

   ____

6. Gift tags are packaged in bags of 8. I have made 367 gift tags for the school fair. How many full bags can I make?

   ____

A sporting problem

1. Unravel the following information and provide the correct calculations to solve each part of this problem. Work systematically through each question, and write down the steps in order.

Mr McGee had a problem. There were four different sporting occasions booked for the same day and he had the job of organising the coaches.

- There were only 3 minibuses that could each carry 18 people and 3 large coaches that could each carry 38 people. Two adults must accompany each bus.
- There were 238 children in the school that day. 56 were going to a football tournament; 27 had been invited to the school athletics event in the next town; 18 were swimming in the swimming gala, and 6 had been picked to try their hand at archery.

a. How many children would be left back at school?

____

____

b. How many adults would be out on that day?

____

____

c. Who should go on which bus?

____

____

Recipe problem

1. **Here is a recipe to make six small sponge cakes. How would you increase the quantities of the ingredients to make 12 or 18 cakes? Complete the table. Remember to keep the quantities of the different ingredients in the same ratio.**

To make 6 small sponge cakes, you will need:	To make 12 small sponge cakes, you will need:	To make 18 small sponge cakes, you will need:
50g soft margarine	_____ g soft margarine	_____ g soft margarine
50g caster sugar	_____ g caster sugar	_____ g caster sugar
1 egg	_____ eggs	_____ eggs
50g self-raising flour	_____ g self-raising flour	_____ g self-raising flour
1 tablespoon cocoa	_____ tablespoons cocoa	_____ tablespoons cocoa
6 paper cake cases	_____ paper cake cases	_____ paper cake cases

SAFETY WARNING: Ask an adult to help you with the hot oven.

Wash your hands before you start. However many cakes you make, the method is the same.

1. Beat the margarine and sugar together in a large mixing bowl until the mixture is smooth and creamy. You can do this with a wooden spoon or an electric whisk.
2. Beat in the egg, a little at a time. If the mixture becomes wet and slimy, beat in a spoonful of the flour.
3. When all the egg has been mixed in, sieve the flour and cocoa into the mixture and stir in gently with a large metal spoon.
4. Place the cake cases in a cake tin and divide the mixture between the cases.
5. Bake in a hot oven at 180°C (or gas mark 5) for 12 to 15 minutes.
6. Your cakes are cooked when they are bouncy and springy to the touch. Leave them to cool on a wire rack. The cakes can be eaten as they are, or with a little icing on the top.

Exchange rates

1. Find out about different currencies around the world. Use the table below to list the countries and currencies you find.

Country	Currency	How much is £1 worth in this currency?

2. How many countries in Europe use the euro? List them below.

____

____

____

____

3. If you received £5.00 pocket money, how much would this be in the following currencies? Try to use a method you can work out easily, such as starting with a smaller amount.

US dollars	
Yen	
euros	

Compare and order fractions

The **denominator** (bottom number of the fraction) tells you how many equal parts that one whole is divided into.

The **numerator** (top number) tells you how many fractional parts there are. You need to look at **both** parts of all the fractions when you are putting them in order of size.

To order fractions that have different denominators, you may find it easier to first convert all fractions so that they have a common denominator.

1. Choose a suitable fraction to complete these number sentences.

a. $\frac{3}{5} >$ ☐ b. $\frac{3}{4} <$ ☐ c. $\frac{2}{3} <$ ☐

d. $\frac{7}{10} >$ ☐ e. $\frac{5}{8} >$ ☐ f. $\frac{2}{10} >$ ☐

g. $\frac{2}{5} <$ ☐ h. $\frac{6}{10} <$ ☐ i. $\frac{3}{8} >$ ☐

j. $\frac{2}{6} <$ ☐

2. Convert these fractions to twentieths and then put them in order, starting with the smallest.

$\frac{3}{5}$ $\frac{15}{20}$ $\frac{7}{10}$ $\frac{2}{10}$ $\frac{2}{4}$ $\frac{2}{5}$ $\frac{8}{10}$ $\frac{1}{4}$

____

3. Convert all these fractions to eighteenths and then put them in order, starting with the smallest.

$\frac{2}{3}$ $\frac{5}{9}$ $\frac{1}{6}$ $\frac{1}{2}$ $\frac{1}{3}$ $\frac{2}{9}$ $\frac{5}{6}$ $\frac{4}{9}$

____

Fraction squeeze

Look carefully at the < and > signs when you complete the number sentences.

For example: $\frac{1}{4} < \frac{1}{2} < \frac{3}{4}$

1. Copy and complete these sentences by squeezing a fraction between the two that are given.

a. $\frac{1}{8} <$ __________ < 1	b. $1 >$ __________ $> \frac{1}{2}$
c. $\frac{1}{2} <$ __________ $< \frac{3}{4}$	d. $\frac{5}{6} >$ __________ $> \frac{1}{3}$
e. $\frac{3}{4} <$ __________ < 1	f. $1 >$ __________ $> \frac{3}{5}$
g. $\frac{1}{4} <$ __________ $< \frac{2}{3}$	h. $\frac{3}{4} >$ __________ $> \frac{1}{4}$

Equivalent fractions and decimals

The fraction $\frac{1}{10}$ is equivalent to the decimal 0.1.

1. Draw a line to link each fraction to its equivalent decimal. Use your knowledge of decimals to do this.

$\frac{1}{10}$	0.5
$\frac{4}{10}$	0.2
$\frac{1}{5}$	0.9
$\frac{2}{10}$	0.75
$\frac{90}{100}$	0.33
$\frac{1}{2}$	0.2
$\frac{1}{4}$	0.5
$\frac{3}{4}$	0.7
$\frac{5}{10}$	0.3
$\frac{1}{3}$	0.4
$\frac{30}{100}$	0.1
$\frac{70}{100}$	0.25

Equivalent shape fractions

Equivalent fractions are fractions that are equal.
For example, $\frac{1}{3}$, $\frac{2}{6}$ and $\frac{4}{12}$ are all equivalent fractions.

1. Shade part of each shape and match the shape fraction to the appropriate number fraction. Draw a line to join each pair together.

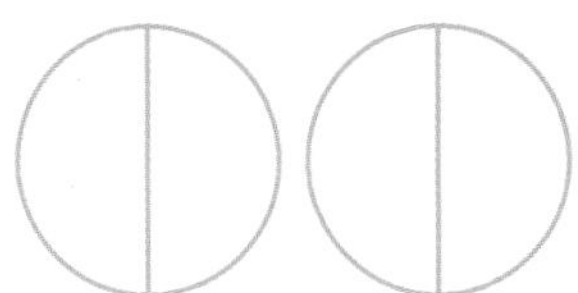
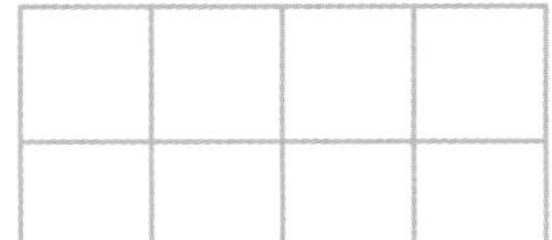

$\frac{2}{5}$ $1\frac{3}{4}$ $\frac{3}{4}$

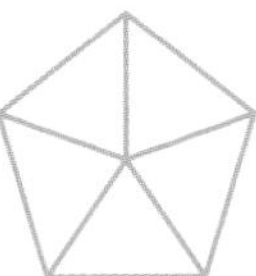

$\frac{1}{2}$

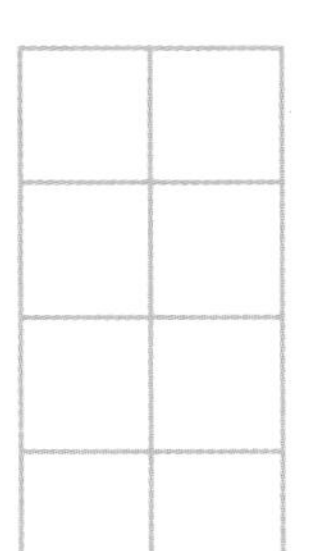

$\frac{5}{8}$ $\frac{3}{2}$ $\frac{15}{10}$

$\frac{3}{3}$ $\frac{7}{5}$ $1\frac{5}{8}$

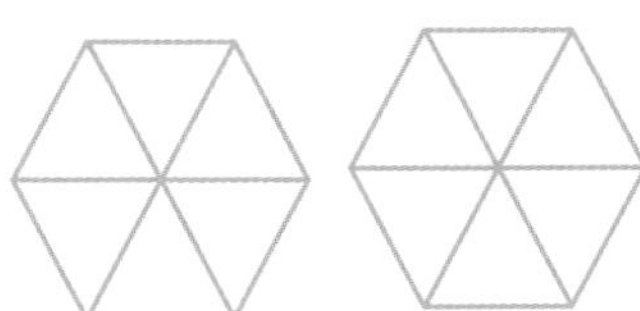

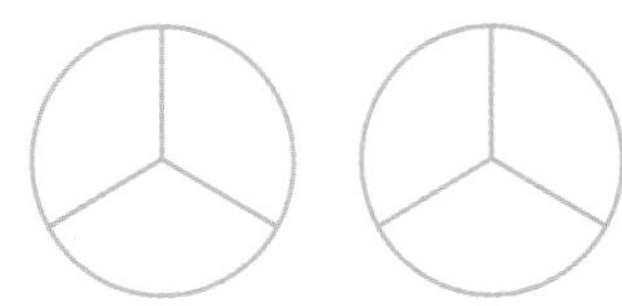

$\frac{13}{8}$ $1\frac{2}{3}$ $1\frac{1}{2}$

$\frac{10}{6}$

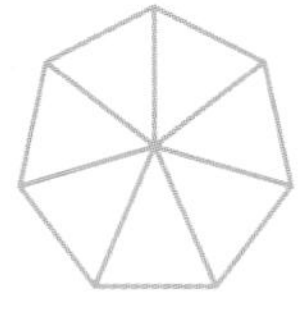
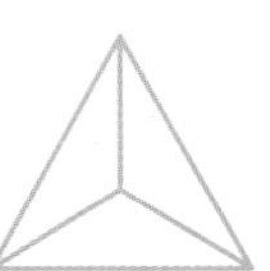
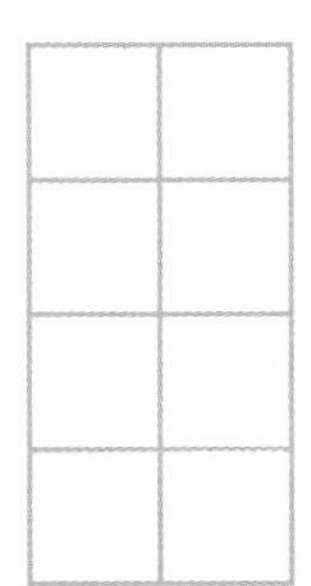
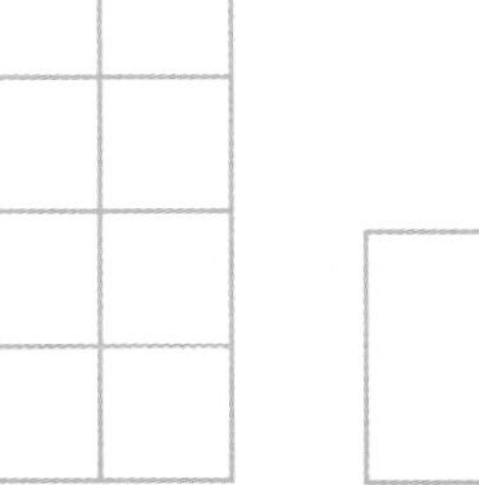
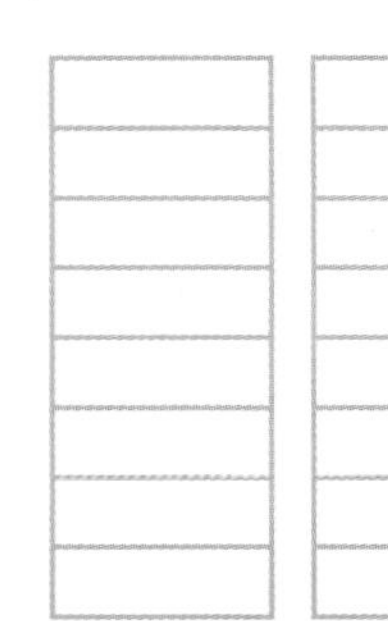
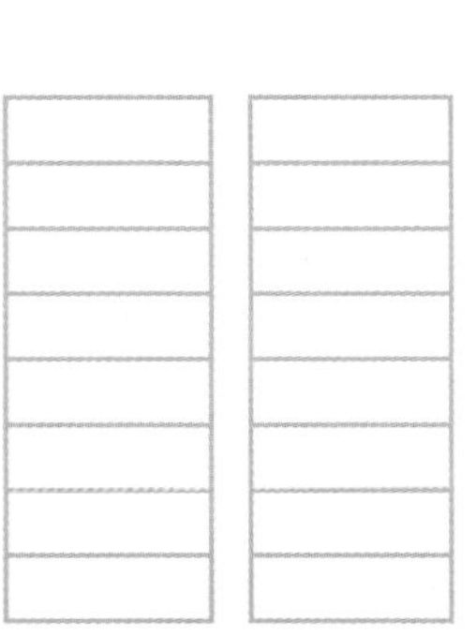
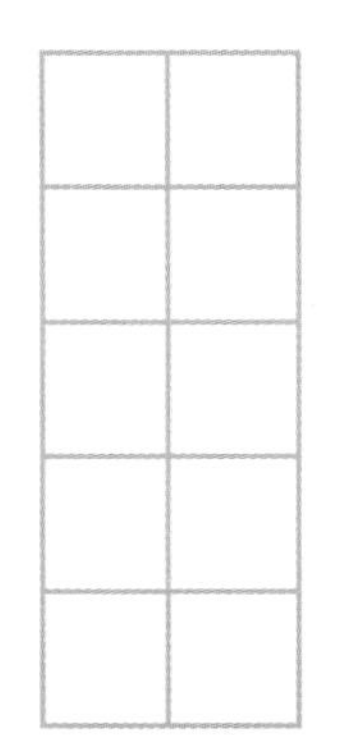
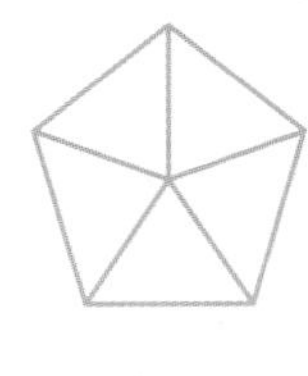
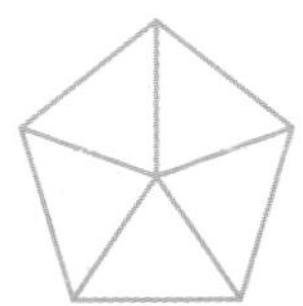

Improper fractions to mixed numbers

A **mixed number** has a whole-number part and a fraction part: $1\frac{1}{3}$, $4\frac{2}{5}$.

An **improper fraction** has a numerator that is bigger than the denominator: $\frac{5}{3}$, $\frac{7}{2}$.

1. For each of these diagrams, write their value as an improper fraction and a mixed number. The first one has been done for you.

a. $\frac{1}{3}$ $\frac{1}{3}$ $\frac{1}{3}$ | $\frac{1}{3}$ $\frac{1}{3}$ $\frac{1}{3}$ | $\frac{1}{3}$

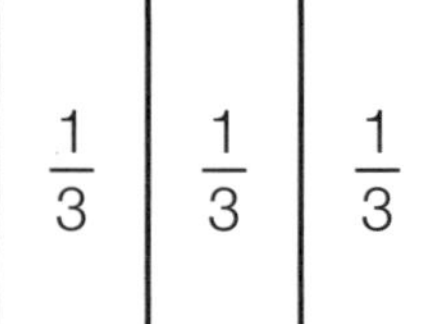

$\frac{7}{3} = 2\frac{1}{3}$

b. $\frac{1}{5}$ $\frac{1}{5}$ $\frac{1}{5}$ $\frac{1}{5}$ $\frac{1}{5}$ | $\frac{1}{5}$ $\frac{1}{5}$ $\frac{1}{5}$ $\frac{1}{5}$ $\frac{1}{5}$ | $\frac{1}{5}$ $\frac{1}{5}$ $\frac{1}{5}$ $\frac{1}{5}$ $\frac{1}{5}$ | $\frac{1}{5}$ $\frac{1}{5}$

____

c. $\frac{1}{2}$ $\frac{1}{2}$ | $\frac{1}{2}$ $\frac{1}{2}$ | $\frac{1}{2}$ | $\frac{1}{2}$ $\frac{1}{2}$ | $\frac{1}{2}$ $\frac{1}{2}$

____

d. $\frac{1}{4}$ $\frac{1}{4}$ $\frac{1}{4}$ $\frac{1}{4}$ | $\frac{1}{4}$ $\frac{1}{4}$ $\frac{1}{4}$ $\frac{1}{4}$ | $\frac{1}{4}$

____

e. 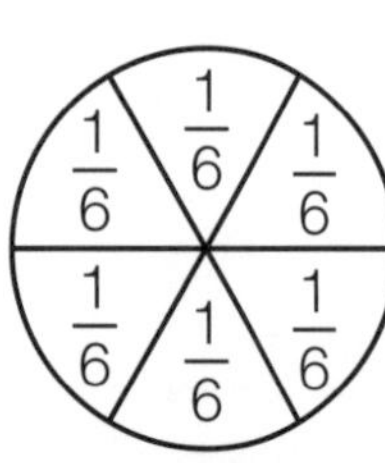

____

To convert or not?

When you add fractions you will sometimes need to convert the answer to a mixed number.
For example: $\frac{3}{5} + \frac{4}{5} = \frac{7}{5} = 1\frac{2}{5}$

1. Convert these improper fractions to mixed numbers.

a. $\frac{13}{5}$ = ____________ b. $\frac{10}{3}$ = ____________

c. $\frac{7}{4}$ = ____________ d. $\frac{16}{9}$ = ____________

e. $\frac{11}{7}$ = ____________ f. $\frac{11}{6}$ = ____________

g. $\frac{51}{2}$ = ____________ h. $\frac{49}{10}$ = ____________

2. Convert these mixed numbers to improper fractions.

a. $7\frac{1}{2}$ =	b. $2\frac{1}{4}$ =
c. $6\frac{2}{3}$ =	d. $4\frac{3}{5}$ =
e. $6\frac{5}{8}$ =	f. $5\frac{6}{7}$ =

Adding fractions with the same denominator

To add fractions with the same denominator just add the numerators:

$\frac{3}{5} + \frac{4}{5} = \frac{7}{5} = 1\frac{2}{5}$

1. Add across and down to complete the grids. Write the answers as mixed numbers if you need to.

a.

$\frac{4}{5}$	$\frac{3}{5}$	
$\frac{7}{5}$	$\frac{3}{5}$	
	$1\frac{1}{5}$	

b.

$\frac{5}{8}$	$\frac{3}{8}$	
$\frac{7}{8}$	$\frac{3}{8}$	

c.

$\frac{3}{4}$	$\frac{6}{4}$	
$\frac{3}{4}$	$\frac{5}{4}$	

2. Complete the pattern.

a. $\frac{1}{4}$, ______________, $1\frac{1}{4}$, ______________, ______________, $2\frac{3}{4}$, $3\frac{1}{4}$, ______________

b. What did you add each time to get the next number? ______________

3. Complete the pattern.

a. $\frac{1}{3}$, ______________, $1\frac{2}{3}$, $2\frac{1}{3}$, ______________, ______________

b. What did you add each time to get the next number? ______________

Subtracting fractions with the same denominator

To subtract fractions with the same denominator just subtract the numerators:

$\frac{5}{6} - \frac{1}{6} = \frac{4}{6}$

1. Subtract these fractions.

a. $\frac{3}{4} - \frac{1}{4} =$ ______________

b. $\frac{6}{7} - \frac{3}{7} =$ ______________

c. $\frac{9}{10} - \frac{5}{10} =$ ______________

d. $1\frac{1}{2} - \frac{1}{2} =$ ______________

2. Subtract across and down to complete the grids. Write the answers as mixed numbers if you need to.

a.

$\frac{4}{5}$	$\frac{3}{5}$	$\frac{1}{5}$
$\frac{2}{5}$	$\frac{1}{5}$	

b.

$\frac{7}{8}$	$\frac{3}{8}$	
$\frac{4}{8}$	$\frac{3}{8}$	

c.

$\frac{9}{4}$	$\frac{3}{4}$	
$\frac{3}{4}$	$\frac{1}{4}$	

3. The difference between two fractions is $\frac{1}{2}$. One of the fractions is $\frac{2}{3}$. The other fraction is a proper fraction. What is it?

____

Add and subtract fractions with related denominators

To work out $\frac{3}{4} + \frac{1}{8}$ we can write $\frac{6}{8} + \frac{1}{8}$ because $\frac{3}{4}$ and $\frac{6}{8}$ are equivalent fractions.

So $\frac{3}{4} + \frac{1}{8} = \frac{6}{8} + \frac{1}{8} = \frac{7}{8}$.

To work out $\frac{5}{6} - \frac{1}{3}$ we can write $\frac{5}{6} - \frac{2}{6}$ because $\frac{1}{3}$ and $\frac{2}{6}$ are equivalent fractions.

So $\frac{5}{6} - \frac{1}{3} = \frac{5}{6} - \frac{2}{6} = \frac{3}{6}$ or $\frac{1}{2}$.

1. Make sure that both fractions have the same denominator before you answer these questions.

a. $\frac{1}{4} + \frac{3}{8} =$	b. $\frac{3}{4} - \frac{1}{4}$
c. $\frac{1}{2} + \frac{5}{6} =$	d. $\frac{1}{2} - \frac{1}{6} =$
e. $\frac{2}{5} + \frac{1}{10} =$	f. $\frac{9}{10} - \frac{1}{5} =$
g. $\frac{1}{3} + \frac{1}{9} =$	h. $\frac{7}{8} - \frac{1}{2} =$
i. $\frac{4}{9} + \frac{2}{3} =$	j. $\frac{11}{12} - \frac{1}{2} =$
k. $\frac{7}{8} - \frac{3}{4} =$	l. $\frac{5}{9} - \frac{1}{3} =$

Fractions challenge

You can use what you know about addition and subtraction being inverses to help with missing number questions. For example:

$☆ + \frac{1}{2} = 1$ $☆ = \frac{1}{2}$ because $1 - \frac{1}{2} = \frac{1}{2}$

1. Work out these questions to find what the star and the question mark stand for. Make sure you give both fractions the same denominator before you solve them.

a.

$☆ - \frac{3}{4} = 0$

$☆ + \frac{1}{4} = ?$

☆ = ________

? = ________

b.

$\frac{1}{3} + ☆ = \frac{3}{6}$

$☆ + ☆ = ?$

☆ = ________

? = ________

c.

$☆ - \frac{1}{4} = \frac{1}{4}$

$☆ - \frac{1}{2} = ?$

☆ = ________

? = ________

d.

$☆ + \frac{1}{2} = 1\frac{1}{4}$

$☆ - \frac{1}{2} = ?$

☆ = ________

? = ________

Multiplying properly!

$\frac{2}{3} \times 3$ means $\frac{2}{3} + \frac{2}{3} + \frac{2}{3}$. This diagram shows that $\frac{2}{3} + \frac{2}{3} + \frac{2}{3}$ is $\frac{6}{3}$ or 2.

1. Use diagrams to help you work these out.

a. $4 \times \frac{1}{5} =$ __________	b. $\frac{2}{3} \times 5 =$ __________
c. $\frac{2}{3} \times 2 =$ __________	d. $4 \times \frac{2}{3} =$ __________
e. $3 \times \frac{3}{4} =$ __________	f. $\frac{3}{7} \times 5$ __________
g. $4 \times \frac{4}{5} =$ __________	h. $7 \times \frac{1}{3} =$ __________

Mixed multiplying!

$1\frac{1}{3} \times 4$ means $1\frac{1}{3} + 1\frac{1}{3} + 1\frac{1}{3} + 1\frac{1}{3}$. This diagram shows that $1\frac{1}{3} \times 4$ is $\frac{16}{3}$ or $5\frac{1}{3}$.

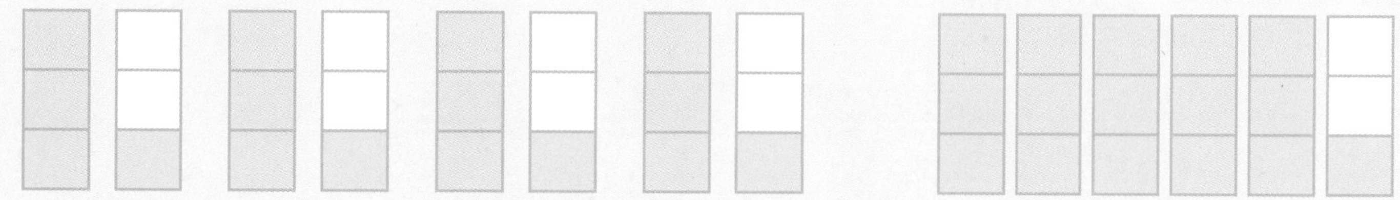

1. Use diagrams to help you work these out.

a. $4 \times 1\frac{1}{2} =$ __________	b. $3\frac{1}{4} \times 3 =$ __________
c. $1\frac{2}{3} \times 4 =$ __________	d. $2 \times 1\frac{3}{4} =$ __________
e. $2\frac{1}{2} \times 5 =$ __________	f. $3 \times 1\frac{4}{5} =$ __________

Decimals: hundredths and thousandths

Each place after the decimal point is a tenth of the value of the place to its left. So the first decimal place is for tenths, the second decimal place is for hundredths and the third decimal place is for thousandths.

10s	1s	.	0.1s	0.01s	0.001s
2	5	·	6	2	3

1. Write the value, in words, of the digit six in each of these numbers. Use the chart above to help you if you need it.

a. 36.775 ______________________________

b. 3.608 ______________________________

c. 21.876 ______________________________

d. 0.462 ______________________________

2. Answer the questions.

a. Which of these numbers is larger than 0.72?

0.712   0.721

____

b. Explain why.

____

____

____

____

Using thousandths

A number with three decimal places is equivalent to a fraction with thousandths, so 0.356 is the same as $\frac{356}{1000}$ or three hundred and fifty-six thousandths.

1. In each star write a decimal number in thousandths that is between the two values given.

a. 4 and 5

b. 1 and 1.23

c. 2.3 and 2.4

d. 0 and 0.2

e. 0.15 and 0.16

f. 9.9 and 10

Rounding and ordering decimals

Decimal numbers can be rounded up to lose 'unwanted' digits.
We round up 'halfway' numbers: 32.5 rounds up to 33.
If the first 'unwanted' digit is 5, 6, 7, 8 or 9, add 1 to the last digit that you keep. Then leave off all the unwanted digits. For example:
6.7**9**5 rounded to the nearest tenth is 6.**8**. The 'unwanted' digits are 9 and 5.

A whole number is a non-decimal number.

1. Round these numbers to the nearest whole number.

a. 34.77 ______

b. 765.51 ______

c. 1329.91 ______

2. Round these numbers to the nearest tenth.

a. 34.24 ______

b. 357.76 ______

c. 1546.05 ______

3. Round these numbers to the nearest hundredth.

a. 34.567 ______

b. 109.109 ______

c. 3102.335 ______

4. Order these decimals on the line below, starting from the lowest number.

34.40 34.09 34.43 34.092 34.015 34.323

____

Decimal sports results

When you put decimals in order, watch out for zero digits.
For example, 3.05m (3m and 5cm) is a shorter distance than 3.50m (3m and 50cm).

A group of children took part in a mini sports session. They each kept their own score card, and are now ready to award points for each event: 5 points for first place; 4 points for second; 3 points for third; 2 points for fourth; and 1 point for fifth.

1. Place the results in order for each event in the spaces at the bottom of the page and award the points.

	Jo	Sam	Jill	Tom	Faarea	David
Long jump	1.90m	2.10 m	2.05m	2.00m	2.15m	1.75m
Standing jump	2.10m	2.05m	1.19m	1.90m	1.98m	1.95m
Bean bag throw	9.65m	9.45m	8.95m	8.65m	9.05m	9.15m
Balance beam walk	3.05m	3.35m	3.65m	3.68m	3.78m	3.60m
Hopped in 30 secs	20.03m	20.30m	21.35m	19.95m	20.35m	23.15m

Results

	Long jump	Standing jump	Bean bag throw	Balance beam walk	30-sec hop
1st					
2nd					
3rd					
4th					
5th					

The overall winner is ______________ because ______________________________.

Three decimal places

When you put decimals in order, remember to watch out for zero digits. For example, 3.005 is smaller than 3.050. Put the decimal numbers on an empty number line to help if you need to.

1. Write the numbers in order, starting with the smallest:

18.811 18.118 81.111 18.181 18.888

____

2. Keiran has tried to put these numbers in order, starting with the smallest.

6.002, 6.202, 6.262, 6, 6.222

a. Which numbers has he put in the wrong place? ____________ and ____________

b. Rewrite the numbers in the correct order.

____

3. Now create your own numbers to put in order. Use the digits 1, 2, 4 and 5 to create six different decimal numbers. Use each digit in every number. Then order your numbers from smallest to largest.

____

____

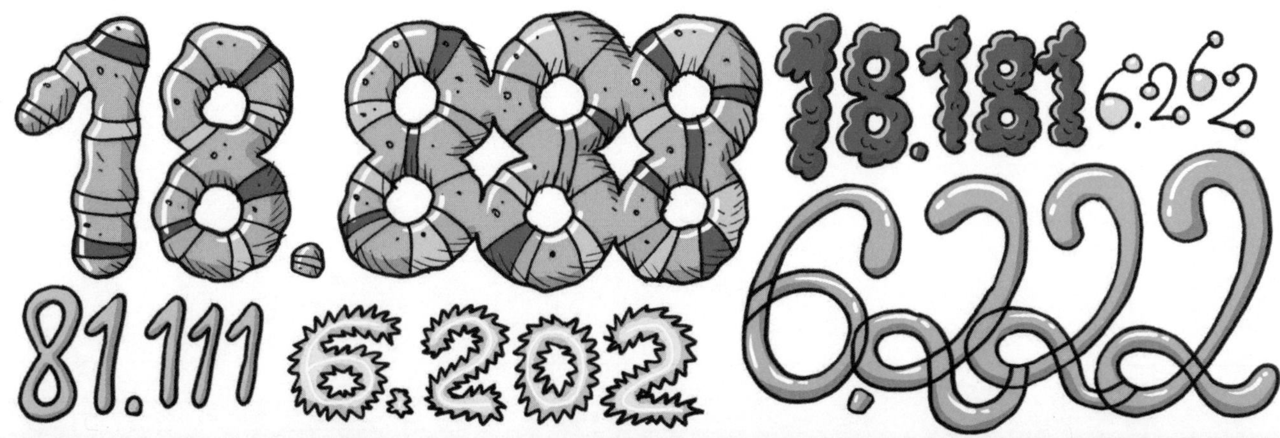

Writing decimal numbers as fractions

Remember that the decimal point separates the whole number part from the part that is less than 1.
The first decimal place is for the tenths. The second decimal place is for the hundredths.

$0.3 = \frac{3}{10}$ $5.3 = 5\frac{3}{10}$ $0.71 = \frac{71}{100}$ $2.71 = 2\frac{71}{100}$

1. In the table below, write the decimal and fraction equivalents. One has been done for you.

Fractions	Decimals
$\frac{1}{2}$	0.5
$\frac{34}{100}$	
	0.25
	0.6
$\frac{3}{10}$	
	0.73
$\frac{99}{100}$	
$\frac{37}{100}$	
	3.89

Fractions, decimals and percentages (1)

Percentage means 'per hundred' or 'in every hundred'. Use this fact to change a percentage to a fraction or decimal: 25% means 25 out of every 100, or $\frac{25}{100}$ or 0.25. $\frac{25}{100}$ simplifies to $\frac{1}{4}$.

1. Draw lines to match the fractions, decimals and percentages that are the same.

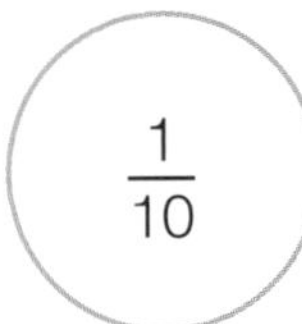

20%

$\frac{1}{4}$

0.1

50%

10%

$\frac{2}{10}$

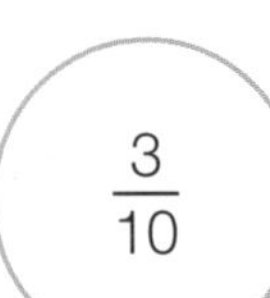

25%

30%

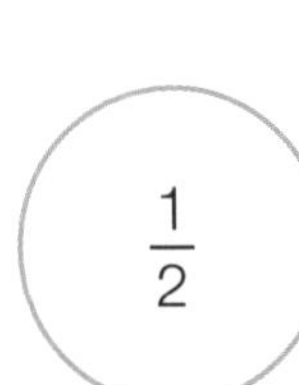

0.75

2. When you have matched all six sets, rewrite each percentage as a fraction with a denominator of 100, and as a decimal, as in the example below.

$10\% = \frac{10}{100} = 0.1$ ____________________

____________________ ____________________

____________________ ____________________

Fractions, decimals and percentages (2)

To change a decimal to a percentage, multiply it by 100.
So, 0.45 as a percentage is 0.45 × 100% = 45%
To find 50% halve the number. To find 10%, divide by 10.

1. Draw lines to link the equivalent decimals, fractions and percentages. One trio has been joined up for you.

0.1	$\frac{2}{10}$	60%
0.2	$\frac{7}{10}$	80%
0.3	$\frac{8}{10}$	90%
0.4	$\frac{1}{10}$	70%
0.5	$\frac{6}{10}$	40%
0.6	$\frac{3}{10}$	50%
0.7	$\frac{9}{10}$	30%
0.8	$\frac{4}{10}$	10%
0.9	$\frac{5}{10}$	20%

2. Draw lines to link the matching amounts. One trio has been joined up for you.

$\frac{1}{2}$ of 30	6	75% of 16
$\frac{1}{4}$ of 80	12	25% of 80
$\frac{1}{5}$ of 35	3	40% of 45
$\frac{3}{4}$ of 16	20	20% of 35
$\frac{1}{10}$ of 60	15	10% of 60
$\frac{1}{3}$ of 9	18	$33\frac{1}{3}$% of 9
$\frac{2}{5}$ of 45	7	50% of 30

Fractions to calculate

To find $\frac{1}{3}$, divide by 3. For example: $\frac{1}{3}$ of £150 = £150 ÷ 3 = £50.

To find $\frac{2}{3}$, find $\frac{1}{3}$ and multiply it by 2. So $\frac{1}{3}$ of £150 = £50 so $\frac{2}{3}$ of £150 = £50 × 2 = £100.

Answer the fraction problems below.

1. Fran shared a box of 48 chocolates with her family. They each had $\frac{1}{6}$. How many chocolates did they have each?

2. I gave $\frac{3}{4}$ of my 108 hair clips to my sister. How many did she receive?

3. $\frac{2}{3}$ of a football crowd have a season ticket. If there are 1221 people, how many have a season ticket?

4. $\frac{3}{5}$ of our school are boys. There are 170 children in our school. How many boys are there? How many girls?

Percentage problems

In a sale you might see a sign that says 10% off. If a coat costs £90, to calculate 10% off find 10% of 90 and subtract:

£90 ÷ 10 = £9, so £90 – £9 = £81.

Another sign might say $\frac{1}{4}$ off. If a shirt costs £24, to calculate $\frac{1}{4}$ off find $\frac{1}{4}$ of 24 and subtract:

$\frac{1}{4}$ of £24 = £6, £24 – £6 = £18.

1. These items are offered in sales in two different shops. Kate wants to pay the lowest prices. Help her calculate which is the cheaper of the corresponding items in each shop. Complete the table below.

Item	Price in Betty's boutique	Price in Garbo	Where should Kate buy?
Dress			
Shoes			
Bag			
Necklace			
Perfume			

Measuring and converting lengths

To convert centimetres to millimetres multiply by 10.
To convert metres to centimetres multiply by 100.
To convert metres to millimetres multiply by 1000.
To convert millimetres to centimetres divide by 10.
To convert centimetres to metres divide by 100.
To convert millimetres to metres divide by 1000.

1. First estimate and then measure the following items. Express your measurements in the suggested units. Then choose three more things to measure and write them in the table.

Length of your garden or building		cm	m
Width of lounge		cm	m
Length of dining table		cm	m
Height of your chair		cm	mm

Converting mass

Remember, there are 1000 grams in a kilogram.

Multiply by 1000 to convert kilograms to grams.

Divide by 1000 to convert grams to kilograms.

Mrs Jones has parcels to send to Australia for her nieces and nephews. She has three empty parcel boxes but each has a maximum weight restriction.

1. Here are the packages that she wants to send. Help her to decide which packages may be sent in which box.

Metric and imperial length problems

Imperial measurements were originally linked to parts of the body. For example, an inch was the width of a man's thumb at the knuckle. People still use imperial measures as well as metric ones; they might say their mass in stones and pounds rather than kilograms, or their height in feet and inches rather than metres and centimetres.

1. Use the chart to help you work out the answers to these problems. The first one has been done for you.

Length

Imperial to metric	Metric to imperial
1 inch (in) = 2.54cm	1cm ≈ 0.4 inch
1 foot (ft) ≈ 30cm	1m ≈ 40 inches
1 yard (yd) ≈ 90cm	1km ≈ 0.6 miles
1 mile ≈ 1.6km	

a. Dwayne throws a cricket ball 10 yards.
How many centimetres does he throw the cricket ball?

10 × 90cm = 900cm. The cricket ball went 900cm.

b. Shanee throws the cricket ball twice as far as Dwayne.
How far does she throw the ball? Answer in metres.

c. Nat's hair is 5 inches longer than her mum's. Her mum's hair is 30cm long.
How many centimetres long is Nat's hair?

d. Keira is 5 feet tall. Her brother Josh is 40cm taller.
How tall is Josh in metres and centimetres?

Metric and imperial mass problems

Originally, any good-sized rock was used to weigh objects. When England started to sell wool to Italy in 1351, the king at the time, King Edward III, declared the stone was fixed at a mass of 14 pounds to make trade fair.

1. Use the chart to help you convert these masses. Write on the labels.

Imperial to metric	Metric to imperial
1 ounce (oz) ≈ 30g	10g ≈ 0.35 ounces
1 pound (lb) ≈ 0.45kg	1kg ≈ 2.25 pounds
1 stone ≈ 6.4kg	

Will
15oz

Samina
50g

Emma
3.5kg

Joe
3lb

2. List the parcels in order, starting with the lightest.

1. __________ 2. __________ 3. __________ 4. __________

3. Look in a cupboard at home or when shopping to find the mass of the following items. Complete the chart. Work out the imperial amount if one isn't on the label.

Item	Mass in metric	Mass in imperial
jam		
flour		
sugar		
rice		
pasta		
baked beans		

Metric and imperial capacity problems

Milk is sold in pints in the USA and sometimes in the UK. A pint is just over half a litre. Petrol is sold in gallons in the USA, but in litres in the UK.

Use the chart to help you work out the answers to the problems.

Imperial to metric	Metric to imperial
1 pint ≈ 0.6 litre	1 litre ≈ 1.75 pints
1 gallon = 8 pints ≈ 4.5 litres	

1. A farmer gives his neighbour Jack 5 pints of milk. Jack trips over and spills half of it. How many litres are left in the jug?

____

A: 2 litres B: 2 gallons

2. a. Which container holds more, A or B?

____

b. How much more in litres?

____

3. Dad buys a 6-pint container of Maddy's favourite drink.
How many litres is that?

____

4. Jayda buys 10 gallons of petrol.
Steve buys 50 litres of petrol.

a. Who buys most petrol?

____

b. How much more do they buy?

____

Ordering masses

Imperial to metric:
1 ounce (oz) is about 30g, and 1 pound (lb) is about 0.45kg.
Metric to imperial:
10g is about 0.35 ounces, and 1kg is about 2.2 pounds.

Find eight different jars and packets in your kitchen cupboards that are weighed in grams, kilograms, ounces or pounds.

1. Put them in order of increasing mass (the lightest first). To do this, you will have to convert them all into the same unit of measurement.
2. Record the masses by drawing and labelling them in the grid.

Remember: ask permission before you do this activity, and don't touch cleaning materials or other chemicals.

1	2
3	4
5	6
7	8

Perimeter

Perimeter is the distance around the outside of a shape. You can use what you know about shapes to find their perimeter without using a ruler to measure every side. For example, a square has four sides of equal length.

1. Measure the sides of each shape (in centimetres) and work out its perimeter.

a.

Perimeter ________________

b.

Perimeter ________________

c.

Perimeter ________________

d.

Perimeter ________________

e.

Perimeter ________________

Area and perimeter

Remember, shapes that have the same area may not have the same perimeter.

1. **Work out the perimeter of each shape in centimetres, using what you know about shapes.**
2. **Work out the area of each shape by counting the squares. Don't forget the part squares. You can match them up to make whole squares.**

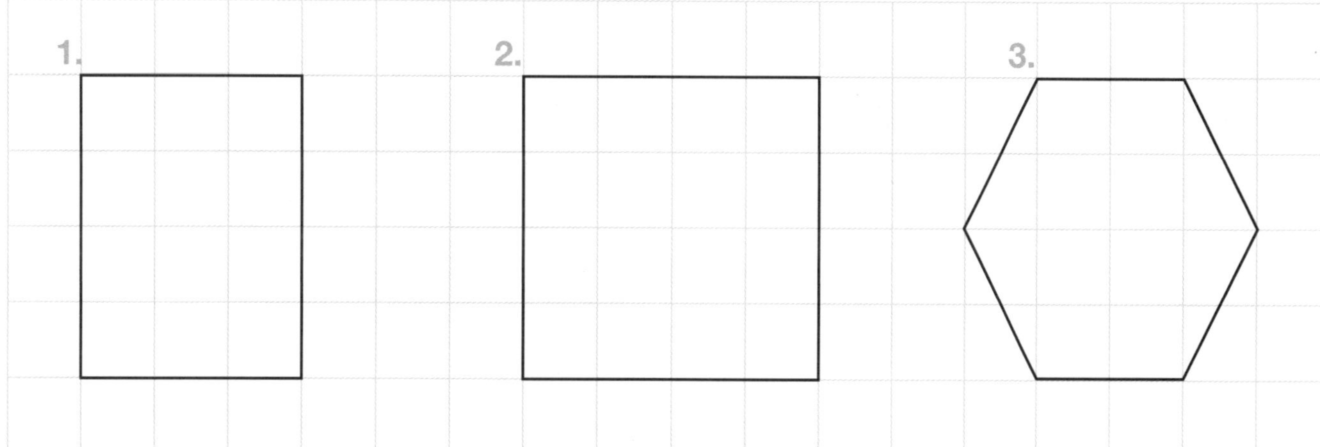

Perimeter ______________ Perimeter ______________ Perimeter ______________

Area ______________ Area ______________ Area ______________

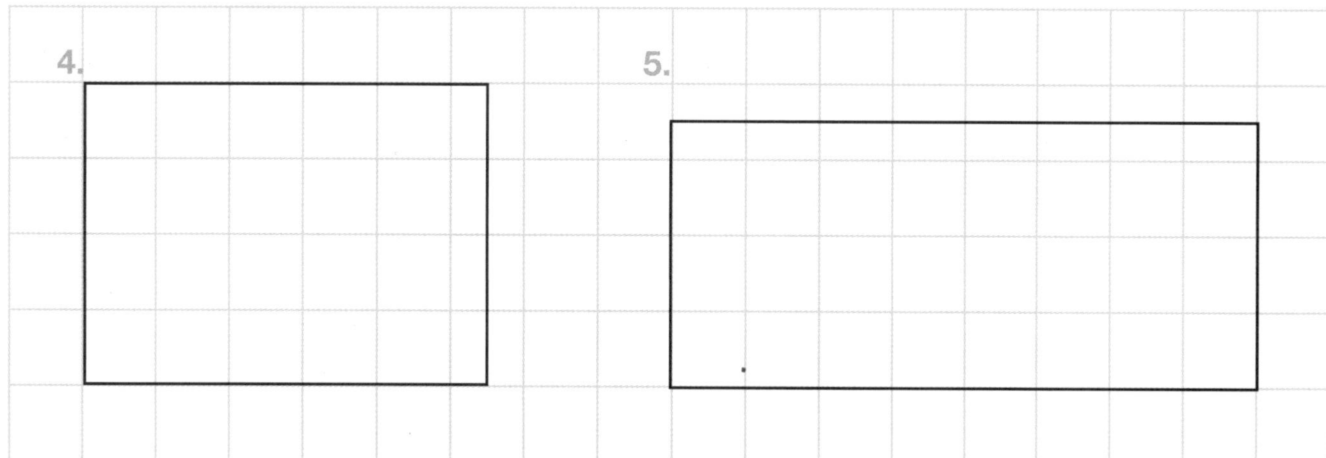

Perimeter ______________ Perimeter ______________

Area ______________ Area ______________

Finding areas

You can find the area of a shape by counting squares on paper or by calculating.
For a rectangle, the formula is area = length × width.
For example, 6cm × 2cm = 12cm² Don't forget the ² which means *squared*.

1. Find the area of these shapes. Look carefully at the units of measurement: you will need to convert some of them.

1. 6cm, 4cm

2. 8m, 5m

4. 10cm, 0.8m

5. 80cm, 0.3m

3. 0.7m, 20cm

6.

0.6m, 40cm

	Area
1.	
2.	
3.	
4.	
5.	
6.	

Living space area

You can find the area of a shape like this by dividing it into two rectangles. Find the area of each rectangle and add them together.

1. Choose a room in your house. Draw a rough plan of its shape in the space below. Leave some space under the plan for writing.
2. Divide the shape you have drawn into squares or rectangles. Measure the length and width of each rectangle and mark these on your plan. It may be helpful to round the numbers to the nearest 10cm for easier multiplication.
3. Now use the length × width formula to find the area of each rectangle. Mark the area of each section on your plan. Use these to calculate the total floor area of your room.

Estimate volume

You can find the volume of cubes and cuboids by counting the number of layers and the number of cubes in each layer.

1. Use small cubes to build two larger cubes and record their volumes.

____________ cube units ____________ cube units

2. Use small cubes to build two cuboids and record their volumes.

____________ cube units ____________ cube units

3. Look at Jon's cube. How many more cubes are needed to make Holly's cube?

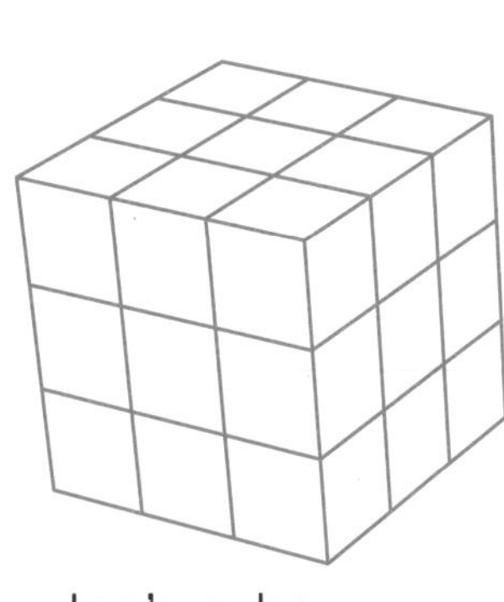

Jon's cube

____________ cubes

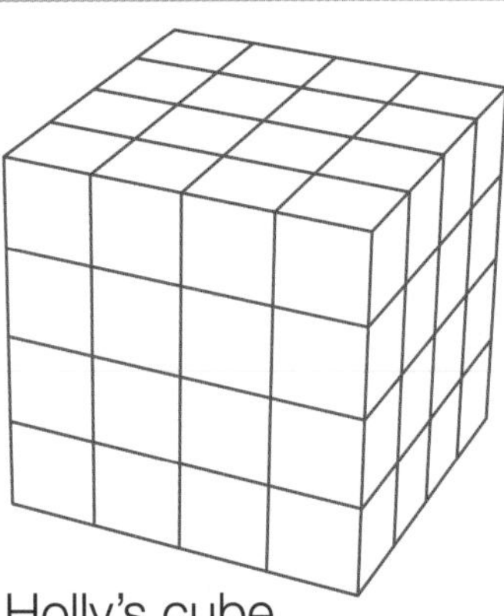

Holly's cube

4. In these diagrams there are no cubes you can't see unless they are needed to hold up another cube.

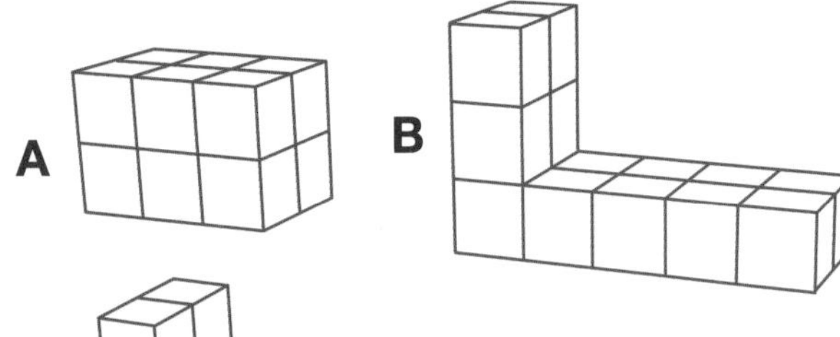

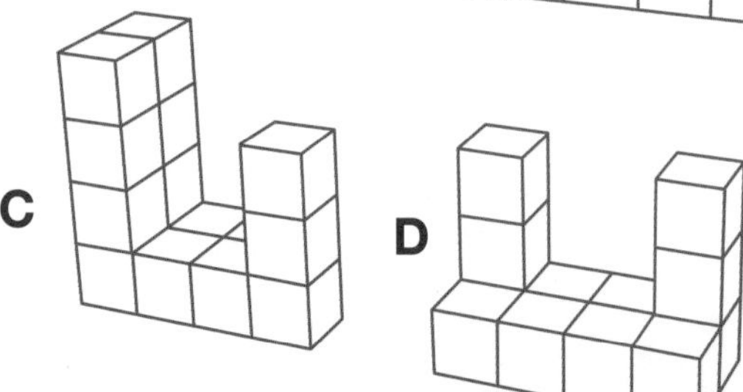

a. Which two shapes have the same volume? ____________________

b. What is their volume?

____________________ cube units

Estimate capacity

There are 1000 millilitres (ml) in a litre (l). Smaller capacities are measured in millilitres. Larger capacities are measured in litres.

Take five different-sized containers and a litre measuring jug. Label the containers A to E.

- **Look at the litre jug. Compare with container A and make an estimate of its capacity. Record it in the table.**
- **Fill container A with sand or water and use the measuring jug to find out how much it actually holds. Record the result.**
- **Do the same for all the containers B to E.**

Container	Estimate	Capacity
A		
B		
C		
D		
E		

1. Which of your estimates was best? Container ______________________

2. Which estimate wasn't so good? Container ______________________

3. Why did you find it hard to make a good estimate of the capacity of this container?

____

____

Activities diary

When you add times, remember that there are 60 minutes in an hour. You could use a blank time line to help if you need to.

1. Keep a diary for 24 hours of the activities given below. Use the recording chart to help. Remember that you may do some things more than once a day.
2. Calculate the time you spent doing these things in a day.
   How long do you think you would spend on them over a week or a month or a year?
   Write these in the table, using an appropriate unit of time.

   For example, if you spend 55 minutes playing football and play three times a week, you would spend 2 hours 45 minutes ((3 × 55 mins) ÷ 60) a week playing football, or 11 hours ((4 × 165 mins) ÷ 60) a month, and 132 hours or $5\frac{1}{2}$ days a year (12 × 11 hours = 132 hours, 132 ÷ 24 = $5\frac{1}{2}$ days).
3. Choose your own activities to add to the table.

Activity	Time	Time spent	Total for 24 hours	Week	Month	Year
Playing football	11:15 – 12:10	55 mins	55 mins	2h 45	11 hours	$5\frac{1}{2}$ days
Sleeping						
Eating						
Washing/ bathing						
Exercising						
Watching TV/using computer						

Using a calendar

Try not to count the days one by one on the calendar! Use the fact that there are 7 days in a week to help you answer these questions quickly. And don't forget, there are 31 days in March and 30 days in April.

1. Use this calendar page to fill in the birthday book using the clues given.

April

Mon	Tues	Wed	Thurs	Friday	Sat	Sun
						1
2	3	4	5	6	7	8
9	10	11	12	13	14	15
16	17	18	19	20	21	22
23	24	25	26	27	28	29
30						

Tom: Monday 16th April

Ellie: Three weeks before Tom ________________

Ben: 13 days after Tom ________________

Alfie: 16 days after Ben ________________

Jane: Three weeks before 1st April ________________

Measurement problems

You may need to convert some of the amounts in a problem so that you are calculating with the same units.

Solve the following problems.

1. My cat weighs 3.1kg and my dog weighs 5900g. How much is their combined mass?

2. Mrs Jones needs 6.8m of fabric for curtains and a further 320cm of the same material for cushions. How much fabric should she buy?

3. On a round trip to work, Mum drives 8km to drop Dan at his friend's house and pick up my friend Ellie. She then takes Ellie and me 5km to school. Finally she drives a further 8420m to her office. How far does she drive to work each day? She repeats the journey on the way home. How far does she drive each day? How far does she drive in a five-day school week?

4. My dad filled his car up at the petrol station. He bought 37 litres of fuel. The next day, he found that the tank was nearly empty because my brother had borrowed the car. Dad was not pleased about having to buy another 32,000ml of fuel. How much fuel had Dad bought in two days? How many litres of fuel had my brother used up?

Summer fete measurement problems

Always read word problems carefully. Decide what calculation to do and write it down. Estimate the answer before you work it out. Check that the answer is about the right size.

Answer the questions about the summer fete.

1. **Guess the weight of the cake!**
   The nearest guess was 3.4kg. The actual weight was 3295g. What was the difference?

   ____

2. **Produce stall**
   Jars of jam cost £2.15 and chutney 25p less. Mrs Giles bought three jars of jam and two of chutney. How much money does she owe?

   ____

3. **Throw the sponge at a teacher! Three sponges for 50p.**
   Rav spent £4.50. How many turns did he have? How many sponges was that?

   ____

4. **Vegetable growing**
   George's marrow was by far the biggest and heaviest at 5.32kg. The nearest competition was Albert's marrow which weighed 425g less. What was the weight of Albert's marrow?

   ____

5. **Egg and spoon race**
   These were the winning times:
   Jane 20.45 seconds **Amy** 21.44 seconds **Sam** 22 seconds
   Sam was 3.8 seconds faster than the person in last place.

a. How much faster than Sam was Jane? ______________________

b. How much faster was Amy than the person in last place?

   ____

School barbecue measurement problems

Remember to include any units in the answer if you are doing word problems that involve money or measures.

The school PTA is organising a school barbecue. They need to calculate how much food to buy, how much it will cost, and how much to charge for each item to ensure they make a profit. They estimate that 500 people will attend.

Use the information in the box to answer the questions below.

500 rolls cost £50.00
500 sausages cost £118.25
500 burgers cost £106.79
500 burger buns £50.00
10 bottles of ketchup cost £32.60
20 bottles of squash cost £48.00

1. How much will 500 hot dogs cost?

___

2. How much will 500 burgers in buns cost?

___

3. How much will 500 burgers in buns and 500 hot dogs cost altogether?

___

4. Add on the cost of the squash and ketchup. What is the grand total spent?

___

5. If they charge each person £3.00, they will take £1500. How much profit will be made?

___

Outdoor pursuits measurement problems

You can estimate the answers to a question first, so that you know whether you need to do the calculation or not.

A group of children are spending the weekend at an outdoor pursuits centre. They have to build a raft to get across a lake.

- The raft can carry a maximum of 170kg.
- Here are the weights of the children: **Izzy** 53.4kg; **Tom** 93.3kg; **Dan** 75.4kg; **Dev** 57.1kg; **Beth** 58.8kg; **Abigail** 61.2kg.

1. Could the raft carry both Tom and Dan?

___

2. Could the raft carry Beth, Izzy and Abigail all together?

___

3. What is the maximum number of children that the raft could take across the lake at one time? Which children are they?

___

4. For safety the children are not allowed on the raft on their own. What combinations could go on the raft in order to get all of the children across the lake?

___

___

Acute, obtuse or right?

An angle is a measure of turn. There are 360° in one whole turn.

An acute angle is less than 90°.	An obtuse angle is more than 90°, but less than 180°. 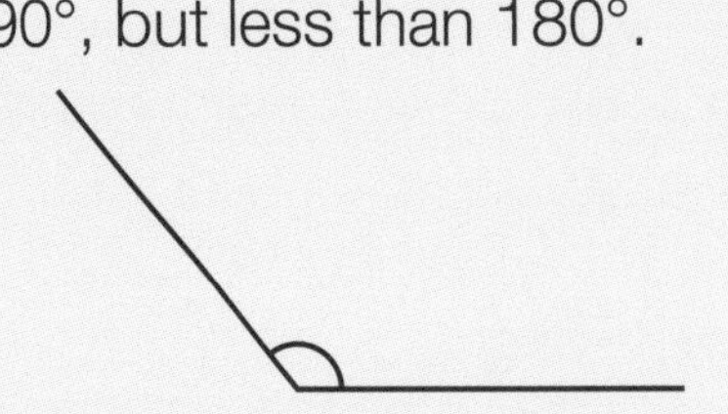	A right angle is exactly 90°. 

1. Label each of these angles either acute, obtuse or a right angle.

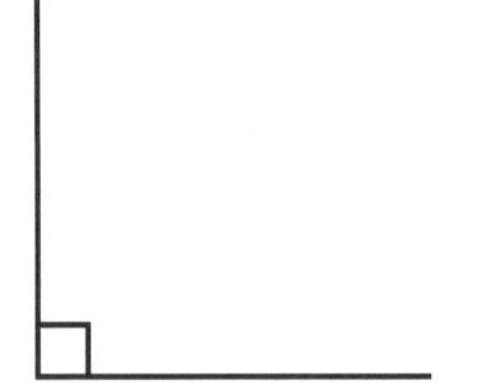

a. ____________________

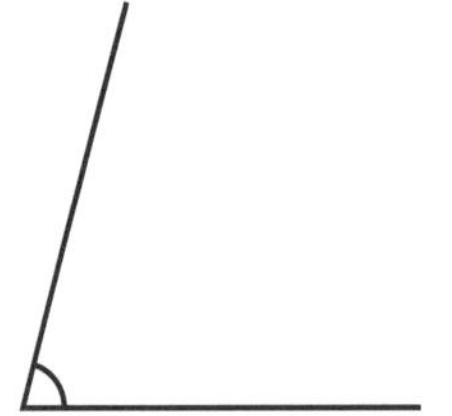

b. ____________________

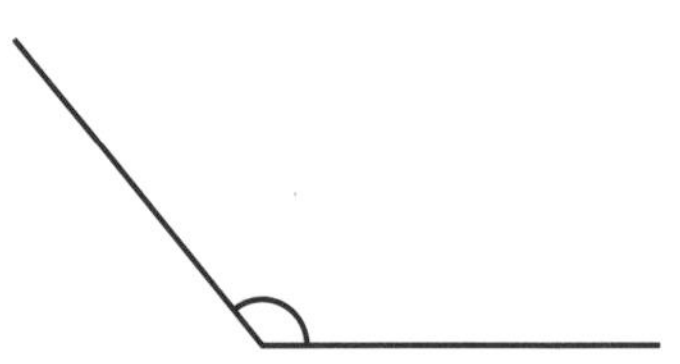

c. ____________________

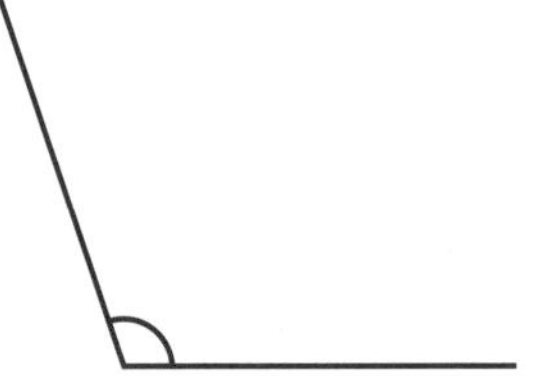

d. ____________________

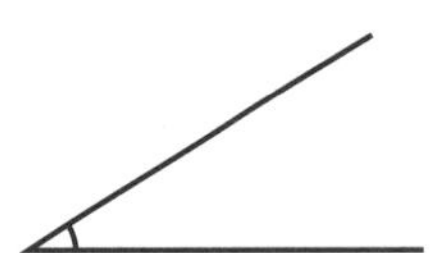

e. ____________________

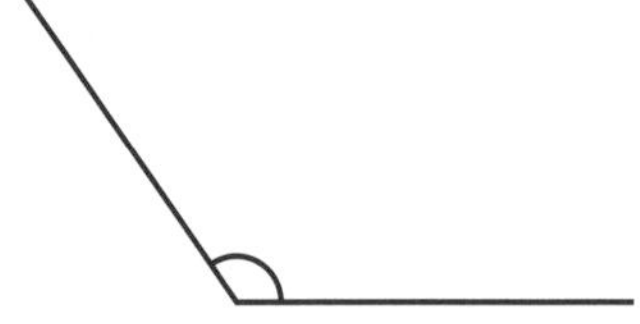

f. ____________________

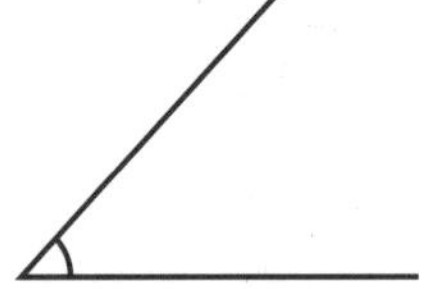

g. ____________________

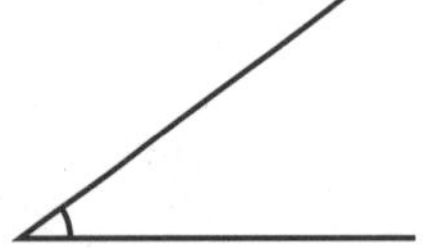

h. ____________________

i. ____________________

What's the angle?

When you measure an angle:

- First estimate its size, or decide if it acute, obtuse or a right angle.
- Line up your protractor correctly.
- Use the correct scale on the protractor.

1. Look closely at these angles. Use your set square or protractor to label them as acute, obtuse or right angles.

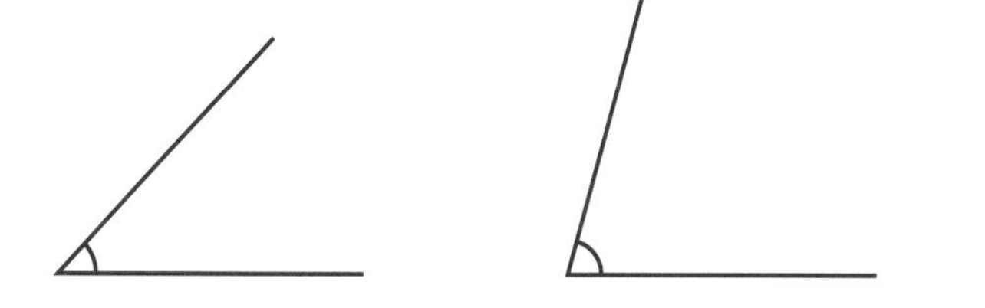

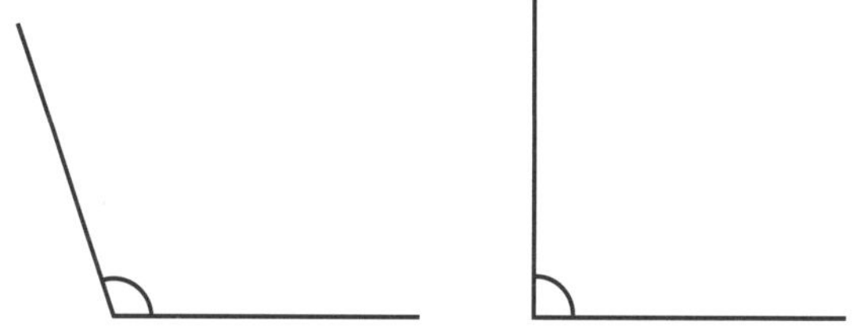

a. ____________ b. ____________ c. ____________ d. ____________

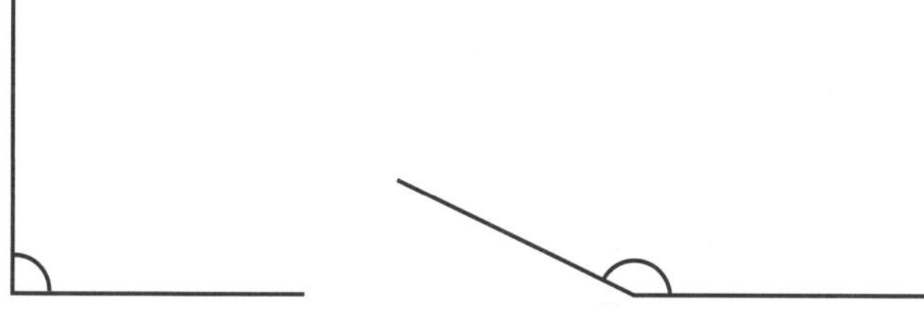

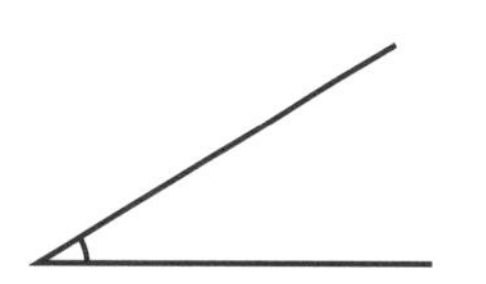

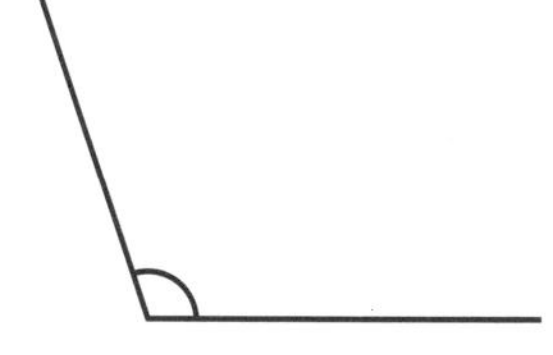

e. ____________ f. ____________ g. ____________ h. ____________

2. Use your protractor to measure these angles as carefully as you can and label them.

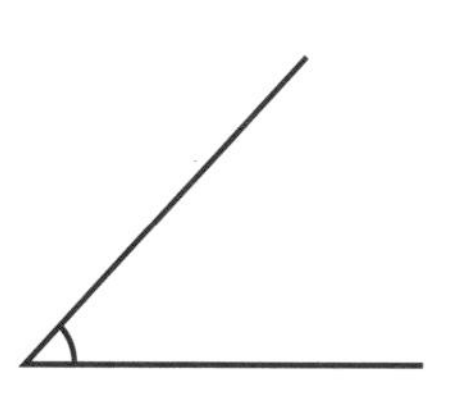

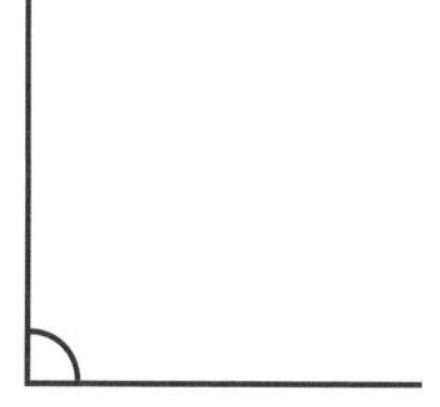

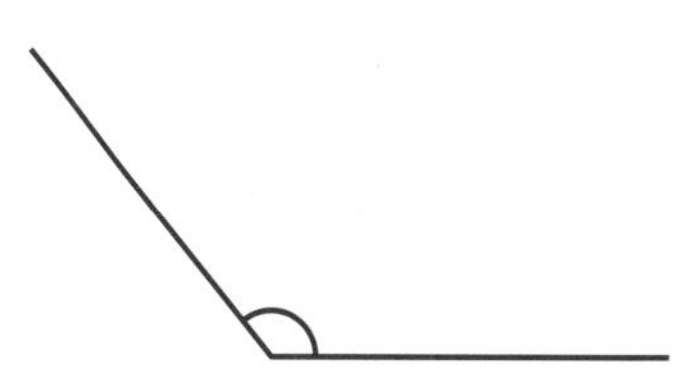

a. ____________ b. ____________ c. ____________

Measuring and drawing angles

To draw an angle of 65°:

- Draw a line.
- Place the protractor at the end of the line.
- Mark a point at 65°.
- Join the end of the line to the point to make the angle.

1. Measure each angle on this triangle as accurately as you can.

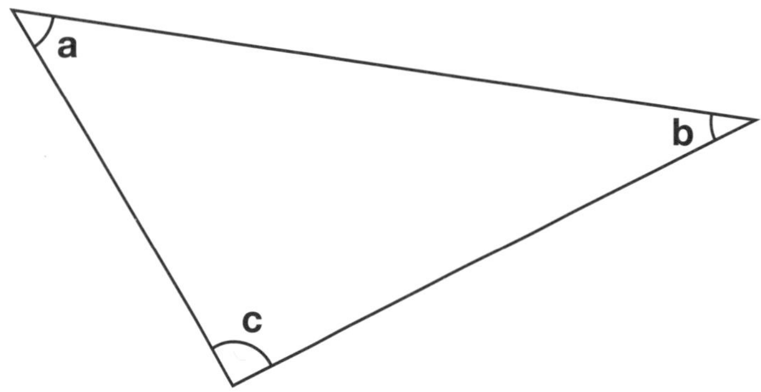

a. Angle *a* ______________ b. Angle *b* ______________ c. Angle *c* ______________

2. Use a ruler, a protractor and a sharp pencil. Draw these angles.

An angle of 55°	An angle of 125°
An angle of 32°	An angle of 270°

Angle rules

One full turn is 360°. The angles at a point add up to 360°.
Half a turn is 180°. The angles on a straight line add up to 180°.

Work out the size of each angle marked with a letter.

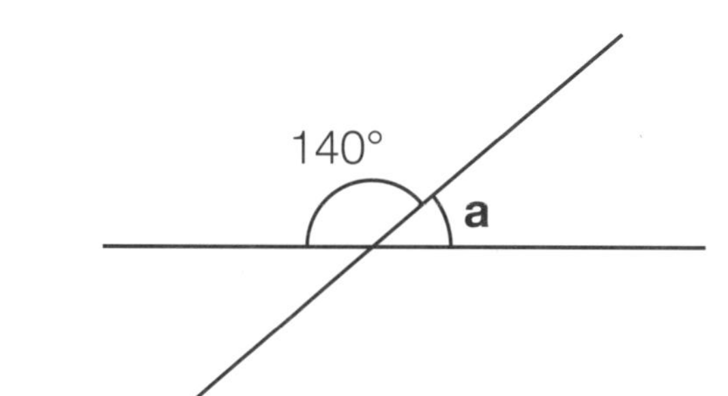

Angle *a* ______________

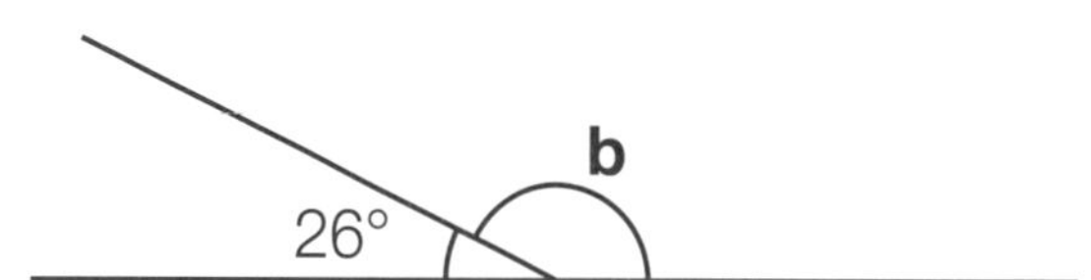

Angle *b* ______________

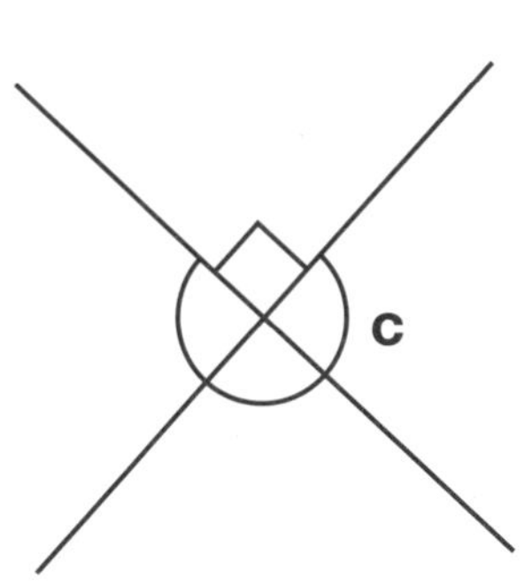

Angle *c* ______________

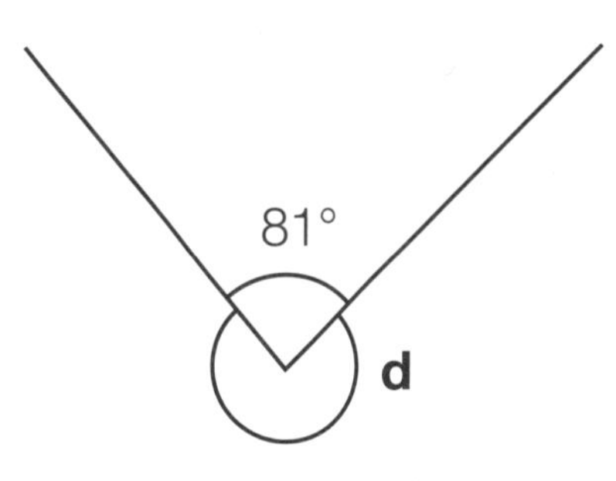

Angle *d* ______________

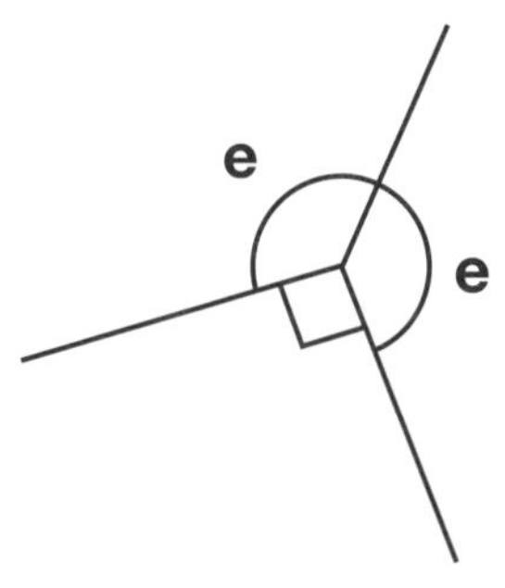

Angle *e* ______________

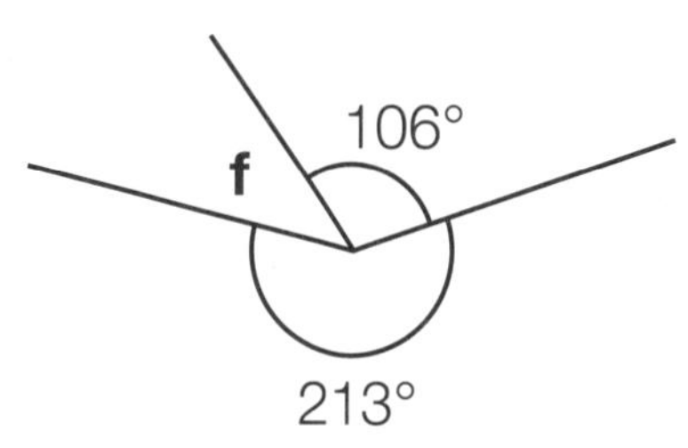

Angle *f* ______________

Missing angles

The angles inside a triangle always add up to 180°.
To find a missing angle in a triangle, you need to look at the angles that you know and subtract them from 180°.

1. Work out the missing angles in these triangles.

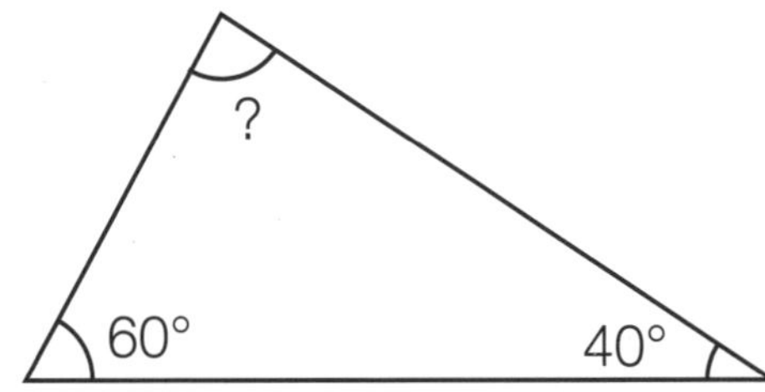

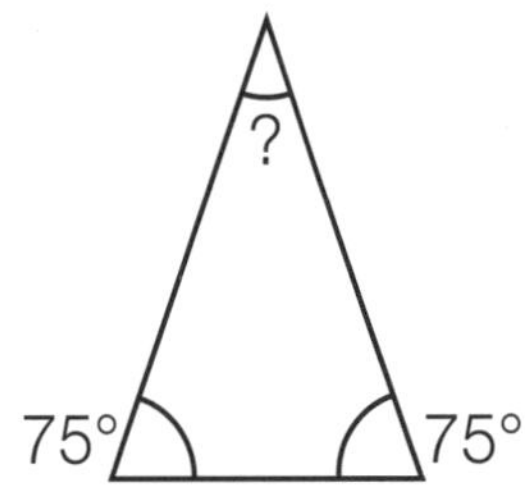

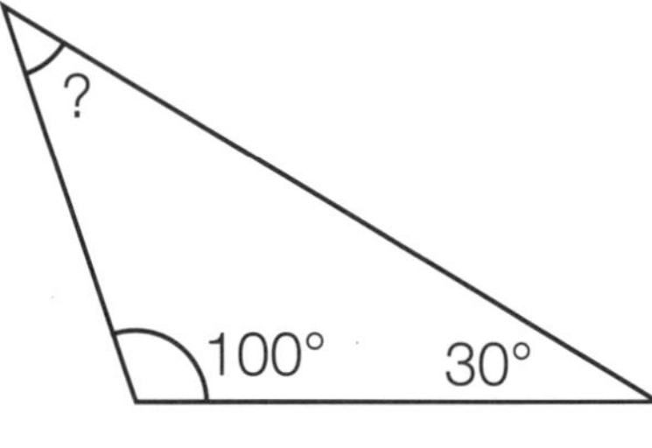

a. ____________________ b. ____________________ c. ____________________

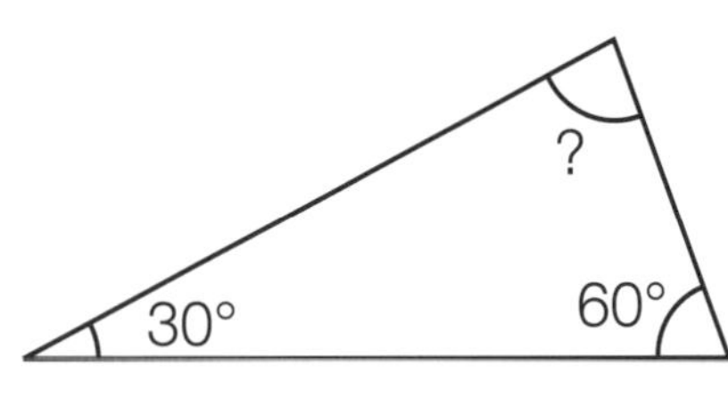

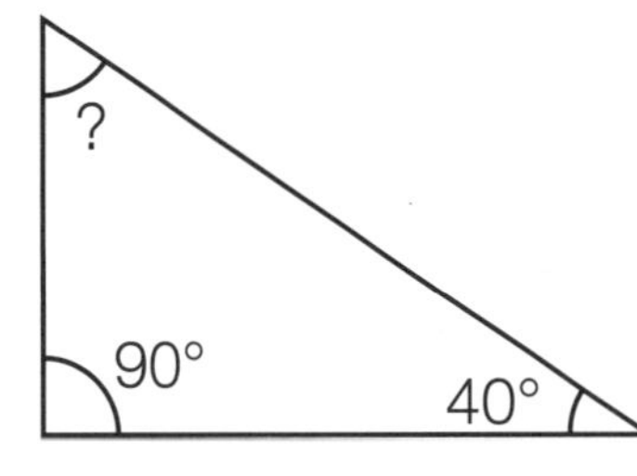

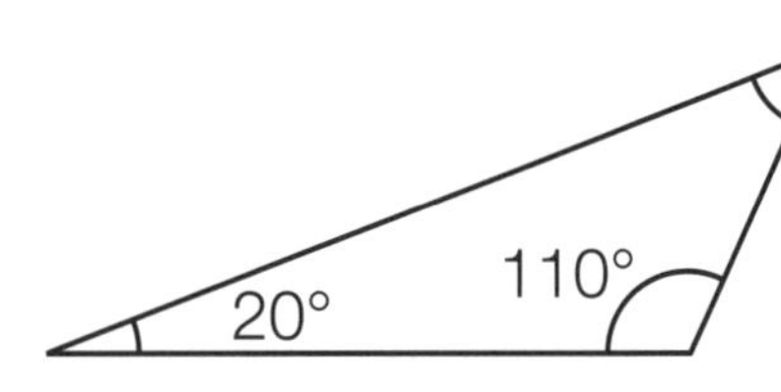

d. ____________________ e. ____________________ f. ____________________

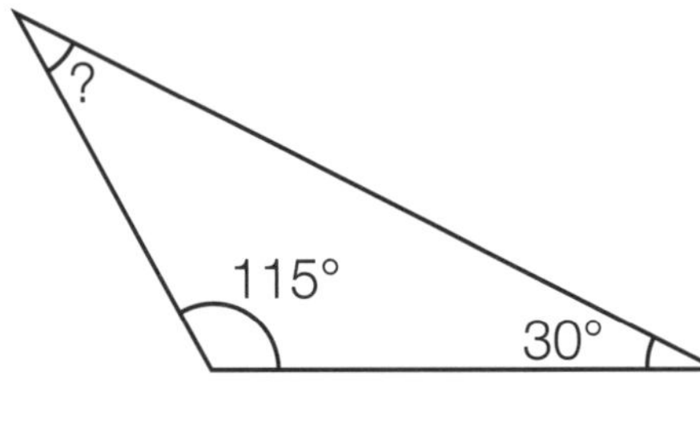

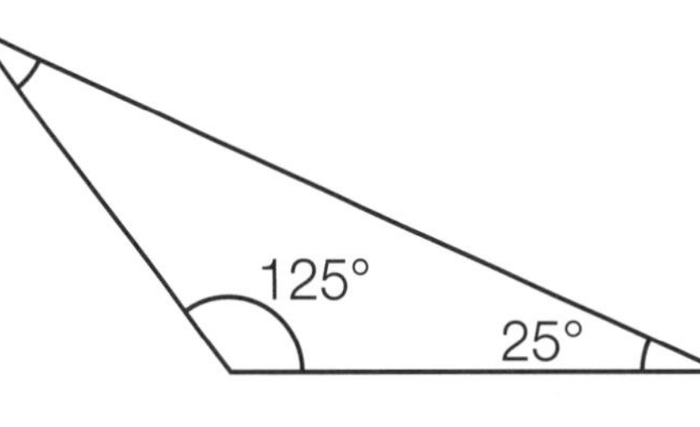

g. ____________________ h. ____________________

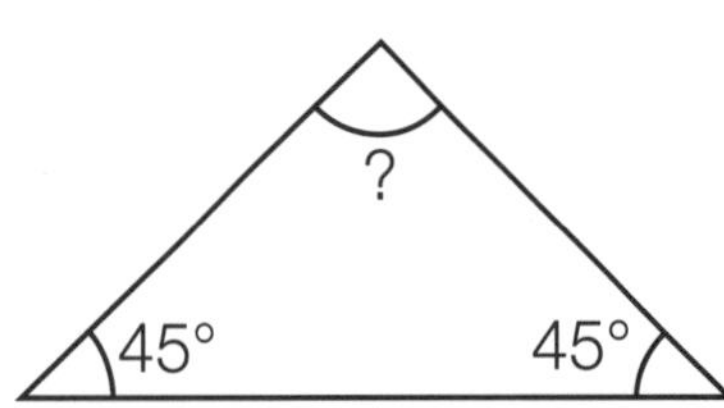

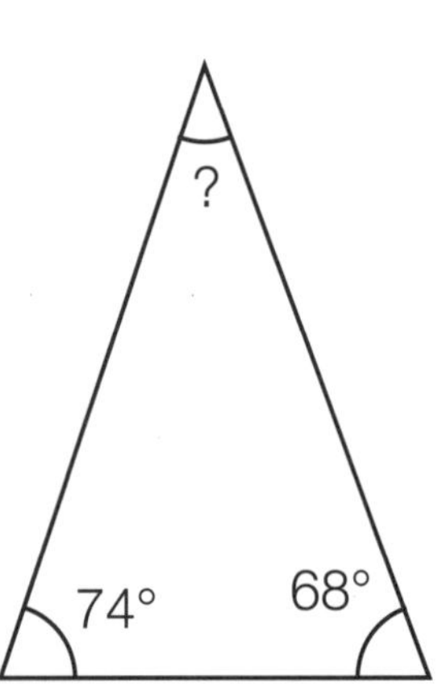

i. ____________________ j. ____________________

Drawing shapes

Remember, you can sketch shapes before you draw them with a ruler. This will help you check that you have used the correct properties.

1. You will need a ruler for this activity. Your challenge is to follow the instructions to draw these shapes. Write the names of the shapes you have drawn underneath.

a. A four-sided shape with no right angles. This is a ________________.	b. A three-sided shape with one right angle. This is a ________________.
c. A five-sided shape with one right angle. This is a ________________.	d. A six-sided shape with three right angles. This is a ________________.
e. A seven-sided shape with four right angles. This is a ________________.	f. A six-sided shape with all angles and sides the same size. This is a ________________.

Shape nets

To work out which nets are correct, choose the base first, then imagine the other faces folded up around it.

Look at these 3D shapes. Next to each shape are two possible nets. However, only one of the nets will form that particular shape. Identify the correct net for each 3D shape, and mark it with a tick.

1. 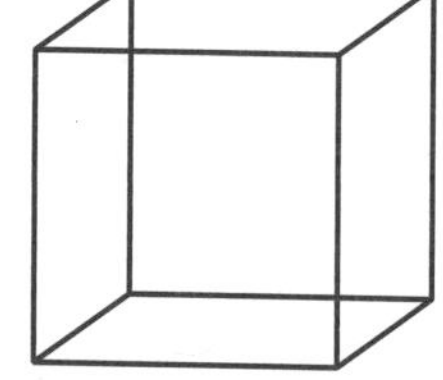

a. 

b. 

2. 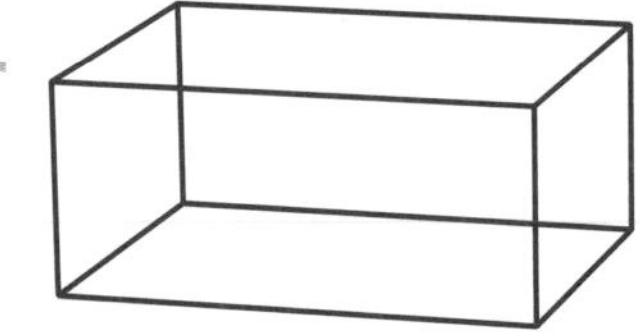

a. 

b. 

3. 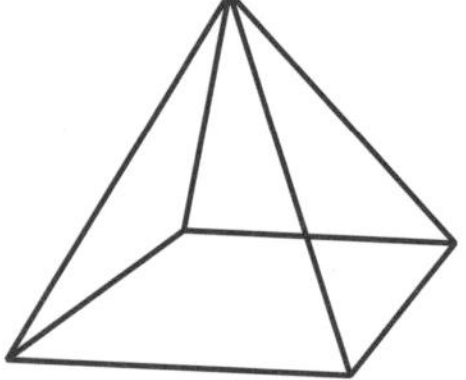

a. 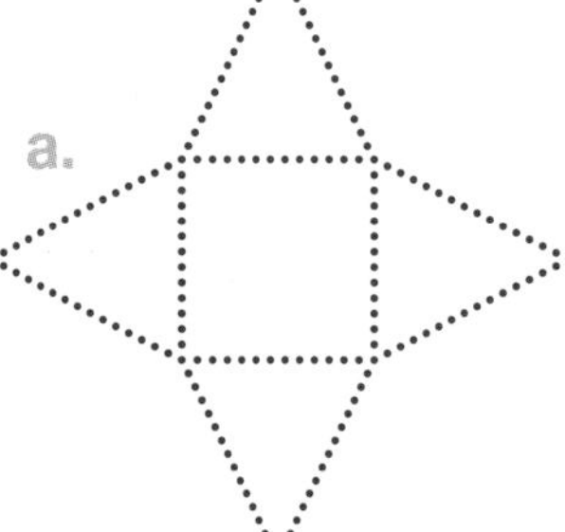

b. 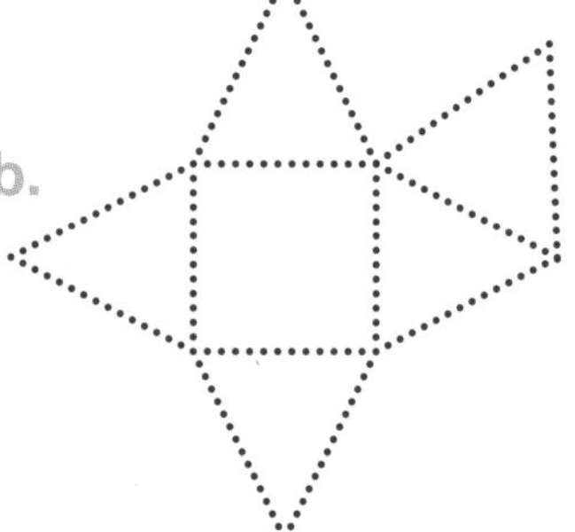

4. 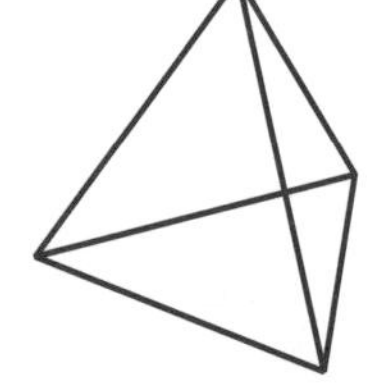

a.

b.

Find what's missing

You can use what you know about the properties of shapes to help you find missing lengths and angles.

1. Draw a rectangle with sides 3cm and 6cm long. Then draw, measure and label the diagonals. Measure and label the angles where the diagonals cross.

2. Repeat the same steps for a square with sides 4cm long.

3. What have you discovered about the angles between the diagonals of a square?

____

4. Diagram ABCD shows a rectangle.

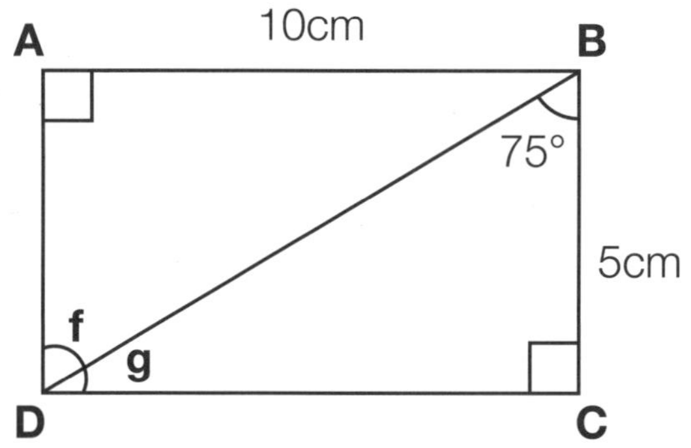

a. What is the size of angle *g*? ____________

b. What is the length of side AD? ____________

c. What is the length of side DC? ____________

Is it a rectangle?

A rectangle is a quadrilateral where every angle is a right angle. Its opposite sides are parallel and equal in length. A square is a special type of rectangle with every side the same length.

1. Look at the shapes and compare them with the description of a rectangle given above. Which of the shapes are not rectangles? Give reasons for your decision.

a. This is ____________________ because ____________________.	b. This is ____________________ because ____________________.
c. This is ____________________ because ____________________.	d. This is ____________________ because ____________________.
e. This is ____________________ because ____________________.	f. This is ____________________ because ____________________.
g. This is ____________________ because ____________________.	h. This is ____________________ because ____________________.

Sorting triangles

Triangles with special properties are: equilateral triangles, isosceles triangles and right-angled triangles. There are also scalene triangles, which can have acute angles and obtuse angles.

1. Look at the triangles below. Colour all the equilateral triangles blue, all the isosceles triangles red and all the scalene triangles green.

2. Write the definitions of the triangles you used.

a. Equilateral ________________________________

b. Isosceles ________________________________

c. Scalene ________________________________

3. Can a scalene triangle also be a right-angled triangle?

____

Reflect it!

When you reflect a shape in a mirror line, the matching points of the object and image are the same distance from the line. The size and shape of the object and image are exactly the same.

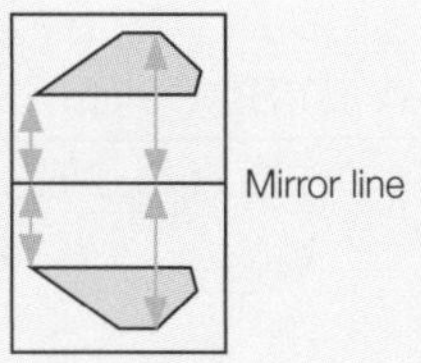

1. Reflect the shapes in both mirror lines. Remember to number each reflected point A1, B1, C1, A2, B2, C2 and so on.

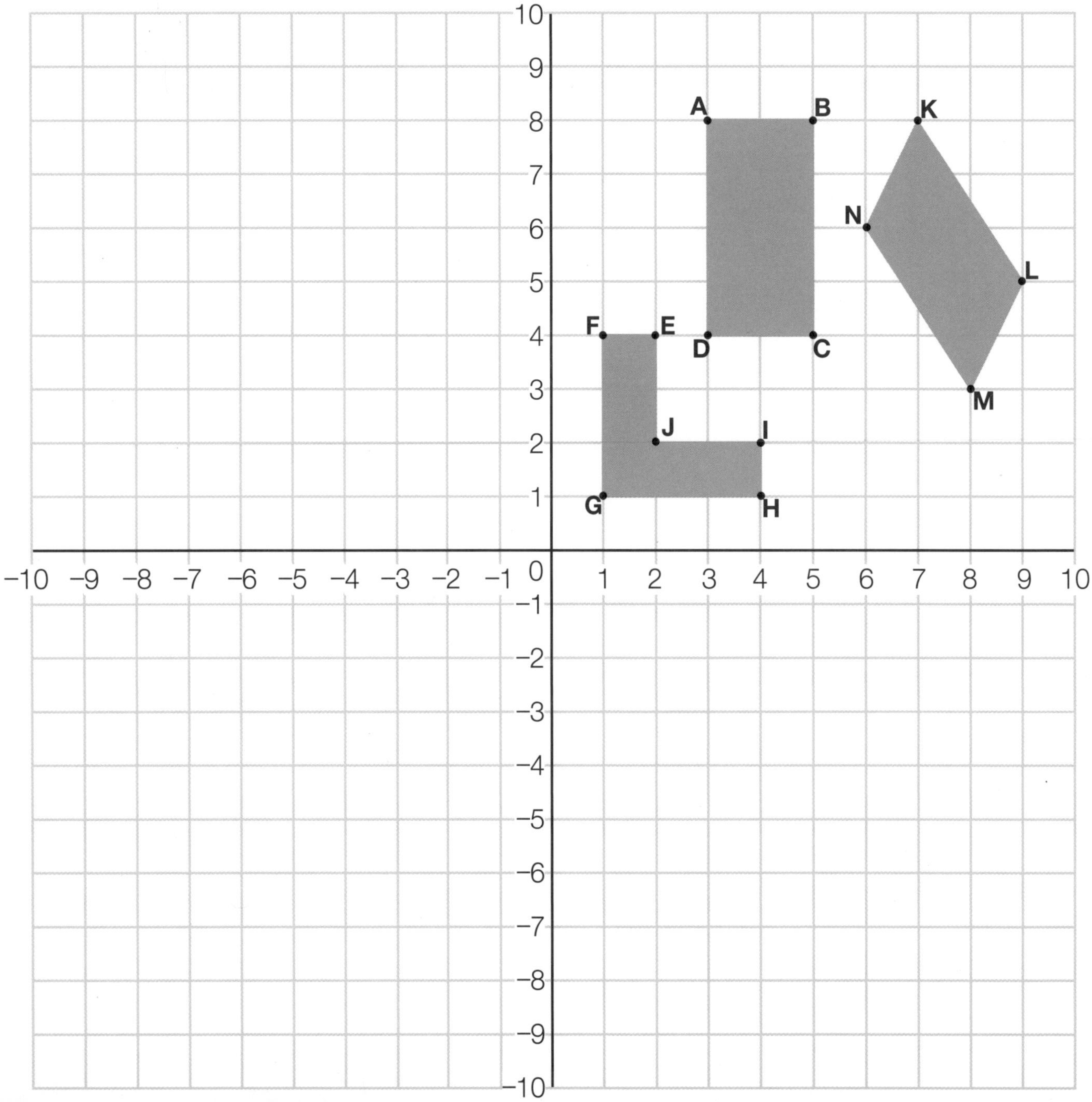

Translate and reflect

When you translate an object:

- Every point of the object moves the same distance in the same direction.
- The image is the same size and shape as the object.

1. Write the coordinates of the points A, B, C, D and E.

   A ______________ B ______________ C ______________

   D ______________ E ______________

2. Join the points to make a shape. Translate the shape eight squares to the left.
3. Then reflect the new shape in the horizontal mirror line.

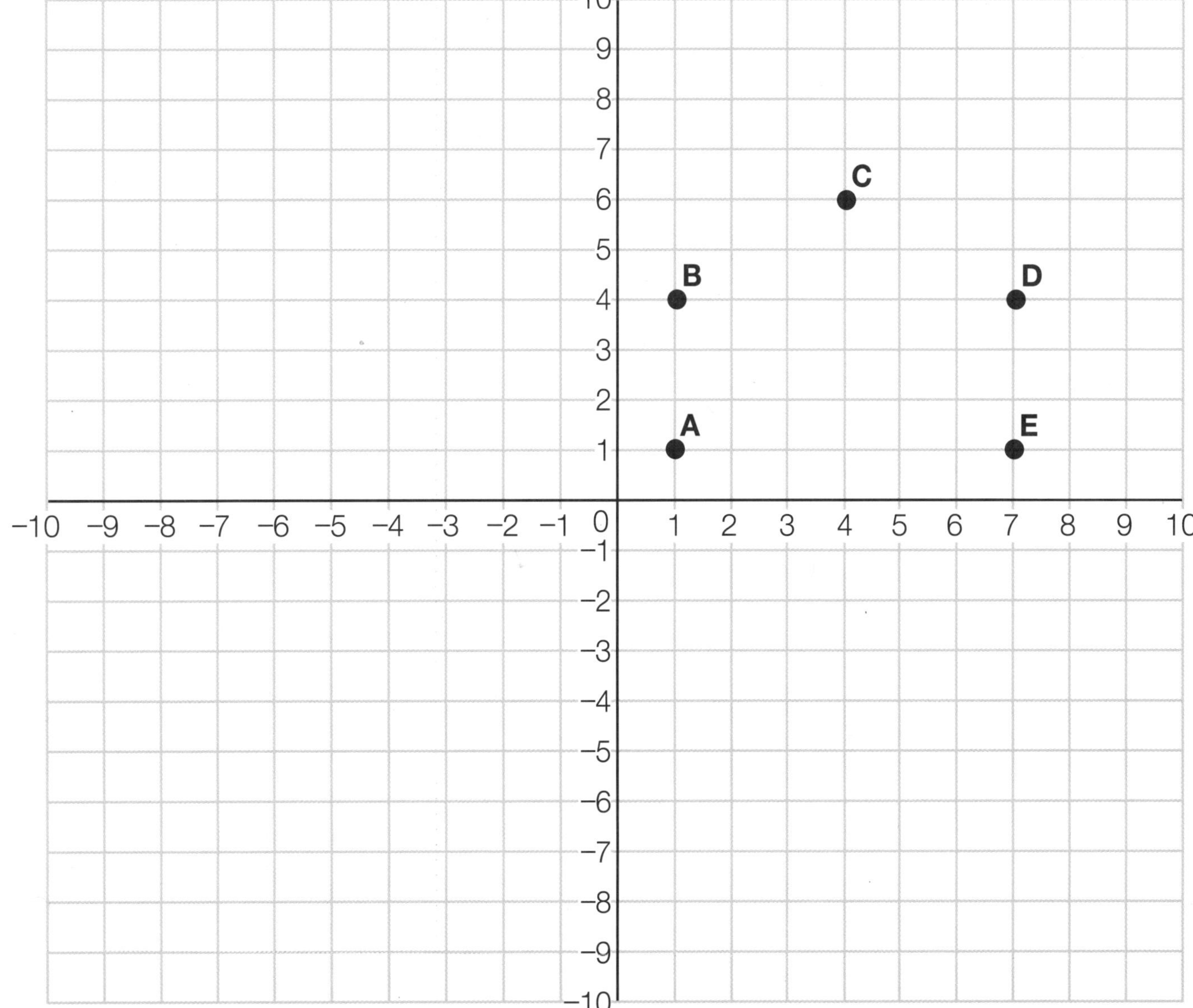

Comparing data

A line graph is a useful way of showing changes over time.
Before you answer questions about a line graph, look at the graph and make sure you understand what it is showing. Look at the title and labels. Make sure you understand the scale.

Look at these two line graphs. They show the temperatures in London and Athens over one 12-hour period in summer.
Use the graphs to answer the questions below.

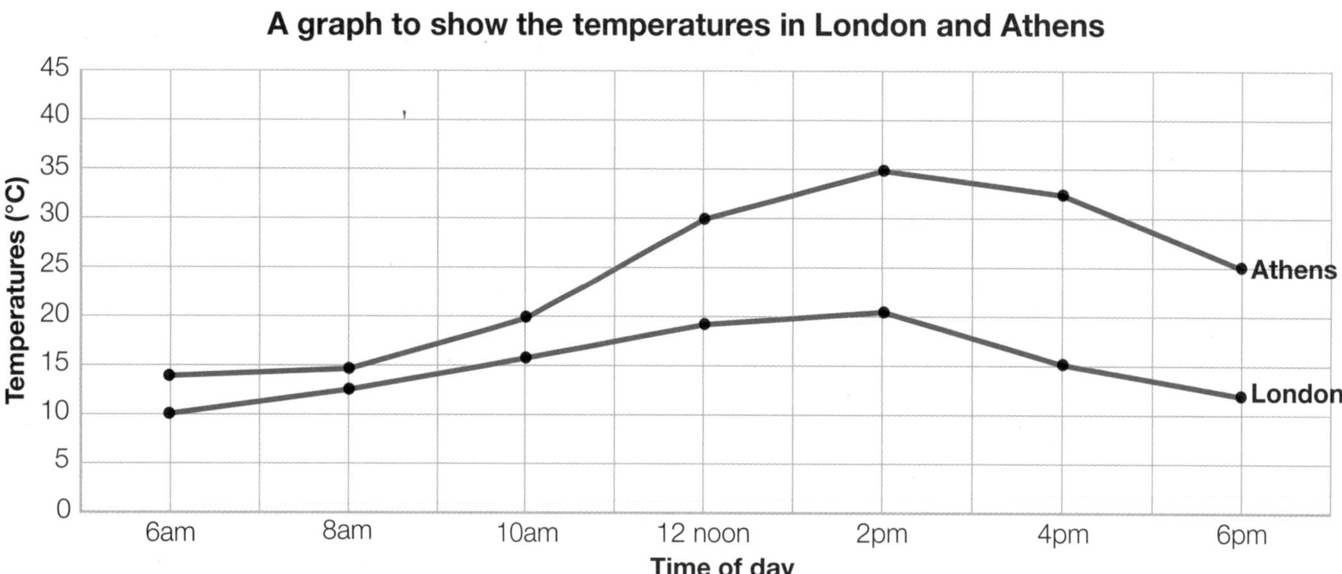

1. What is the difference between the highest temperatures shown in Athens and London?

___

2. What is the difference between the highest and lowest temperatures in London?

___

3. What is the temperature in each city at 5:00pm? ___

4. Why is this information displayed as a line graph, not a bar chart or a bar line graph?

___

___

___

Missing data

When you are completing a bar chart, make sure that you know what the scale is on the frequency axis and use this to fill in the missing data. Look at the other bars to help work out the height of the bar.

Complete these graphs from the information provided, then answer the questions.

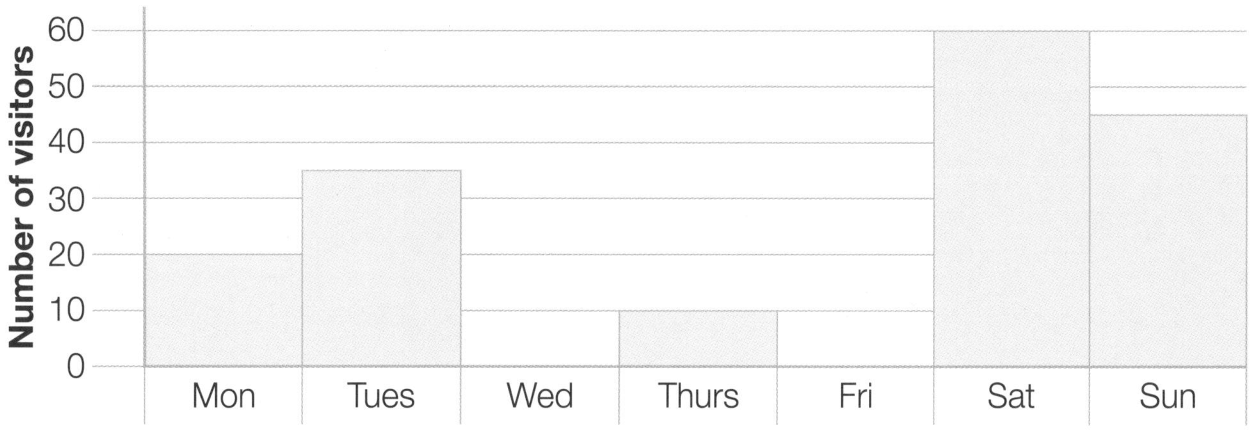

1. There were 35 visitors on Wednesday. Draw the bar to show this.
2. There were 42 visitors on Friday. Show this information on the graph.
3. What was the total number of visitors to the website that week? ______________________

Line graph to show the temperatures in my garden on a day in July

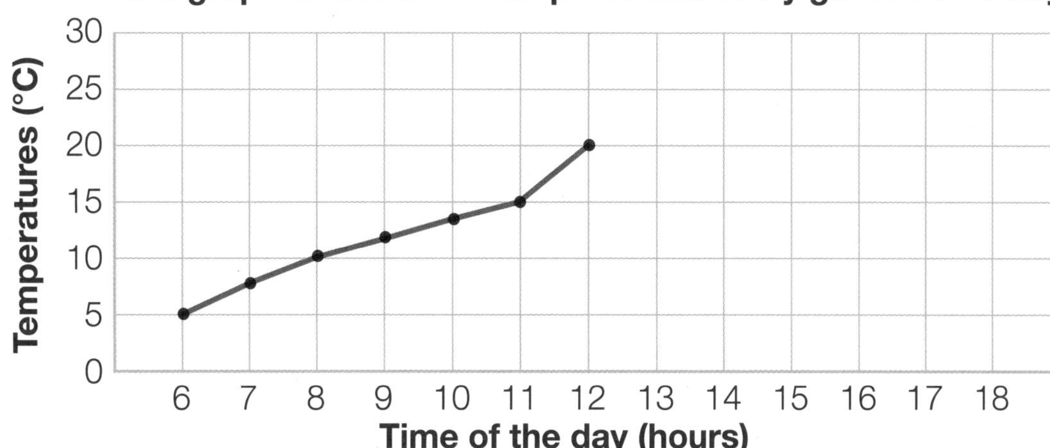

Time	Temp (C°)
13.00	21
14.00	22
15.00	21
16.00	21
17.00	18
18.00	16

4. Complete the graph by adding the data shown in the table (see above right).

Complete a timetable

To work out a time interval, count on from the start time to the end time. You could use a blank time line to help you.

Here is part of a timetable which is being considered for trains between Norwich and Liverpool. Study it carefully and then try to answer the questions below.

Norwich							12.52	13.49	**a.**	15.53	16.57	18.45	19.30	20.51
Thetford							13.19	14.16	**b.**	16.20	17.24	19.12	19.57	21.18
Ely							13.49	14.47	**c.**	**f.**	17.51	19.46	20.22	21.46
Peterborough							14.28	15.25	**d.**	17.15	18.30	20.25	20.55	22.20
Grantham							14.57	15.58	**e.**	17.49	19.05	21.00	**n.**	22.55
Nottingham	09.12	10.36	11.45	12.35	13.33	14.38	15.34	16.44	17.32	18.33	19.45	21.40	22.10	23.35
Chesterfield	09.52	11.13	12.20	13.17	14.17	15.16	16.16	17.20	18.12	19.13	20.15	**I.**		
Sheffield	10.15	11.37	12.39	13.37	14.37	15.35	16.36	17.42	18.35	19.25	20.35	**j.**		
Stockport	11.22	12.24	13.25	14.23	15.33	16.23	17.23	18.26	19.23	20.23	21.17	**k.**		
Manchester Piccadilly	11.37	12.37	13.37	14.37	15.37	16.37	17.37	18.37	19.37	20.32	21.28	**l.**		
Liverpool Lime Street	12.22	14.25	14.25	15.24	16.25	17.25	18.25	19.25	20.25	**g.**	**h.**	**m.**		

1. How long does the first train from Nottingham take to reach Liverpool Lime Street?

2. What is the shortest journey time from Nottingham to Liverpool Lime Street?

3. Use the times between stations to complete this section of the return journey from Liverpool Lime Street to Nottingham.

Liverpool Lime Street	12.00
Manchester Piccadilly	
Stockport	
Sheffield	
Chesterfield	
Nottingham	

4. There is a proposal to extend the train service. The boxes with letters on the timetable on the previous page represent when the extended service will run. Use other entries in the timetable to estimate suitable times for the new service. Write your estimates below.

a. ________ b. ________ c. ________

d. ________ e. ________ f. ________

g. ________ h. ________ i. ________

j. ________ k. ________ l. ________

m. ________ n. ________

Jay wants to travel by train from Exeter to meet the 15.37 at Manchester Piccadilly. Use the internet to find the times and details of his best journey.

____

____

Line graph problems

Remember to read the times and numbers on each axis carefully when you enter the data on to a graph.

The petrol in the tank of a lorry was measured every hour. These are the measurements. Input this information on to the line graph below.

Time	10:00	11:00	12:00	13:00	14:00	15:00
Volume of petrol	50 litres	30 litres	20 litres	20 litres	5 litres 50 litres	35 litres

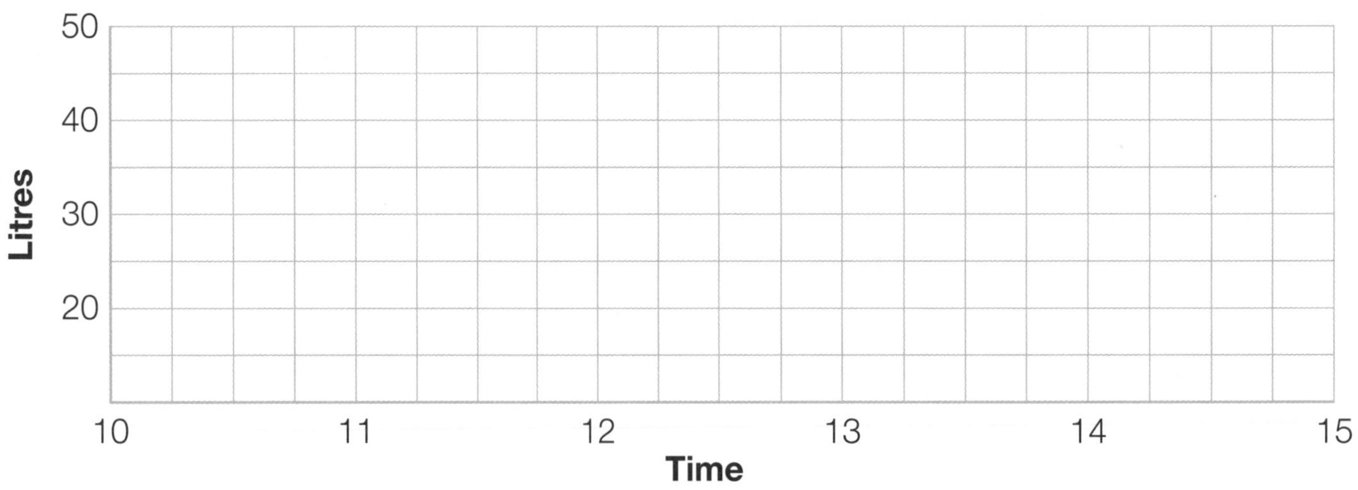

Now use the graph to answer these questions.

1. How much petrol was in the tank at 11:30? __________

2. At approximately what time was the petrol at 10 litres? __________

3. What do you think happened between 12:00 and 13:00? (Check how much petrol was used and why that might be.)

____

4. What happened at 14:00? __________

5. How much petrol was used in the last hour of the journey? __________

Every graph tells a story

1. Look at the line graph below. What story do you think it is telling?
2. Give the graph a title and label the axes.
3. Write the story. Start by completing the sentence starter, then continue.

At _________ o'clock ________________________________.

Then ______________________________

Tip: There is a clue in the sentence starter that the graph involves times, so use that to help you label one of the axes.

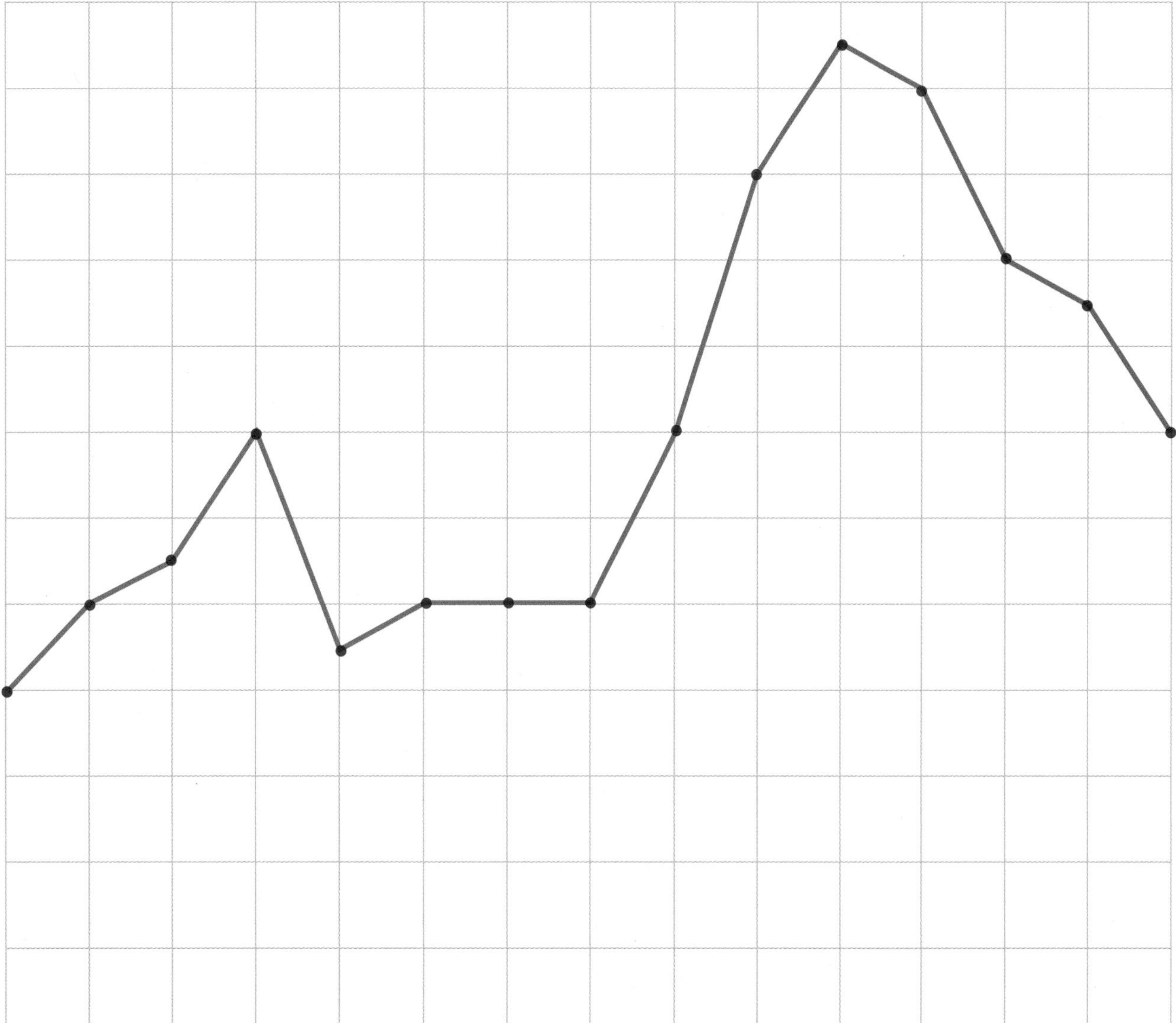

Progress chart

Making progress? Tick (✔) the cogs as you complete each section of the book.

	Most questions completed	All questions completed
Number and place value	○	○
More practice?		
Addition and subtraction	○	○
More practice?		
Multiplication and division	○	○
More practice?		
Calculation problems	○	○
More practice?		
Fractions, decimals and percentages	○	○
More practice?		
Measurement	○	○
More practice?		
Geometry: properties of shapes	○	○
More practice?		
Geometry: position and direction	○	○
More practice?		
Statistics	○	○
More practice?		

WELL DONE!

YOU DID IT! ★

Name: ______________________

You have completed

YEAR 5 MATHS

Practice Book

Age: __________ Date: __________

Index